MOM
to
MOM

MOM
to
MOM

Commonsense
Tips and Advice
Every Mom
Needs to Know

GLORIA G. ADLER

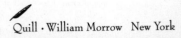

Quill · William Morrow   New York

It is the policy of William Morrow and Company, and its imprints and affiliates, recognizing the importance of preserving what has been written, to print the books we publish on acid-free paper, and we exert our best efforts to that end.

Library of Congress Cataloging-in-Publication Data

Adler, Gloria.
Mom to mom : commonsense tips and advice every mom needs to know / Gloria G. Adler.
p. cm.
ISBN 0-688-15793-9
1. Parenting—United States.   2. Child rearing—United States.
3. Mother and child—United States.   I. Title.
HQ769.3.A35   1998
649'.1—dc21   97-32782
CIP

Printed in the United States of America

First Edition

1 2 3 4 5 6 7 8 9 10

Book Design by Leah Carlson

www.williammorrow.com

CONTENTS

INTRODUCTION

The best parenting advice comes not from your pediatrician, Dr. Spock, or a recent article in a parenting magazine. The best — and surely the wisest — parenting advice comes from mothers just like you and me. Mothers who have been stuck on the interstate with an infant in tow who's got a very messy diaper; mothers who have had to contend with not just one obstreperous teenager but two at the same time; mothers who have figured out how to shower, shop, clean, feed, read, and not fret at the same time; mothers who know how to get their kids to eat their vegetables; mothers who have tried-and-true secrets for family airplane travel; mothers who know what the fine balance is between being a homework helper and homework prodder for their kids; mothers who know how to save money on food, clothes, toys, and supplies. Moms just like you and me.

Parenting experience is of great value, and nothing compares with the experiences of hundreds of mothers.

Mom to Mom offers tips on everything from breastfeeding techniques and bottlefeeding, dealing with teenagers' dating, teaching your toddler his home phone number, to turning ordinary objects into toys, infant and toddler safety, discipline, and more. In compiling *Mom to Mom* I heard from parents around the country and the world (thanks, in part, to the Internet), so there's a wide range of incredibly useful tips, techniques, advice, and stories, the kind I wish I had had when I was raising my two children.

Mom to Mom is a book that you can read from cover to cover or flip through as you need particular advice. It will be one of the most useful parenting tools you have. I think you will be comforted by knowing that no matter what problem or concern you have, somebody else has encountered and solved that problem first. For nearly every problem, *Mom to Mom* has a solution.

I hope you have as much fun reading *Mom to Mom* as I did compiling it. It was truly a joy talking with (and e-mailing) parents from all over. But above all, enjoy your parenting years.

—Gloria G. Adler
New York

LIST OF
CONTRIBUTORS

Carol Almond
Denise Lapachet Barney
Melissa Benton
Gayle Bice
Kellie Brown
Trish Brunkhart
Lisa Bugg
Terri Burris
Amanda Chan
Jodi Chapman
Susan Cohen
Shelly and Paul Dalton
Loretta M. DeLuca
Margaret Demarco
Kathy Dettwyler
Karin Dietterich
Anne Dupont
Brenton Eckert
Nancy and James Elliot
Lori Evans
Daniella Farrington

Andrea Felkins
Scott Fisher
Barbara Gage
Heather Garven
Margaret Gold
Ellen Goodridge
Mary Gordon
Rachel Hamlet
Maria Heil
Roberta Henry
Karen Holloway
Eileen Horvath
Marie Houck
Christine Insell
Enid Yvonne Karr
Martha Kaufman
Ligaya Kelly
Brenda Kim
Nancy Krauss
T. Lamkin
Valerie Lauterbach

Julie Liss
Ron Low
Kelly Luellen
Melinda McKnight
Rhonda Maguire
Diane Malowney
Katherine E. Maus
Ginger Miranda-Feldman
Julie Misa
Carmelo Montalbano
Dale Morgan
Julie Orofino
Marjorie Peskin
Kristin Portello
Dawn Price
Muthiah Ramamoorthy

Paul Redmond
Tracy Riench
Cynthia A. Rohrbeck
Nancy Shargool
Gail Sikkenga
Lisa Stewart
Anna Stuttard
Marcy Thompson
Judy Tigay
Wendy W.
Marilyn Walker
Liza Wasser
Diane Kimble Willcutts
Rosemarie Toni Wiseman
Alison Wyld
Ruthann Logsdon Zaroff

MOM
to
MOM

BATH TIME

Bath time can be one of the most precious and the most harrowing experiences a parent can have. Moms share their stories of bath time trauma and also their tips about how to make this activity easier for the whole family.

You really don't need to buy a special bath seat to keep your baby properly positioned in the bathtub. Once she's outgrown a baby basin and can sit up on her own, you can use a regular plastic laundry basket. It's less confining (some babies are afraid of having their legs lowered into the water and through the leg holes of one of those special bath seats), it allows the baby to splash around, and it keeps all bath toys within the baby's reach.

After the bath, I always lay my baby on a waterproof crib pad on the floor. While he's on it, I dry him and let his diaper area air out (this helps prevent diaper rash, my pediatrician told me), but if he should pee or poop while he's there, it doesn't soak through to the floor.

My sister told me that one of my nieces had this fear of going down the drain. Apparently Mr. Rogers (of *Mr. Rogers' Neighborhood*) has a song that addresses this fear. The chorus goes, "You won't go down the drain, no, you won't go down the, won't go down the, won't go down the drain . . ." It worked.

I love Mr. Rogers.

When my kids were little, they hated having the shampoo rinsed out of their hair. They were scared the soap or water would get in their eyes, but they just wouldn't hold their heads back! It finally got to the point where I didn't even *try* to wash their hair in the bathtub at all. The only way that didn't turn into a major screamfest (on both our parts) was to use the kitchen sink. I would put a towel on the counter and let them lie on it with their heads hanging over the sink. They were looking toward the ceiling. Then I'd wash their hair and pour cups of clear water over it until they were rinsed. Later, I got one of those sprayer things and simply sprayed their heads. They liked this method, and it made things a lot more peaceful at our house!

BEDTIME

Bedtime can reveal the most rewarding aspects of parenthood as well as our most impatient sides. A child can make it very easy or very, very difficult! Sometimes there is no substitute for experience. If one mom is stumped by a child's behavior, only another mom, with similar troubles, can provide the answer. When dealing with a situation as precarious as bedtime, moms need all the advice they can get.

My young son liked the feel of my robe when I was giving him his last bottle of the night, and he would cry as soon as I laid him down in his crib. To help him sleep better throughout the night, I bought a robe of the same material and made a little throw blanket for him. We call it his "mommy blanket," and I tell him that even when I've left the room, he knows he's not alone.

Something that I would suggest to all moms is keeping a bedtime ritual for their child. You can include a bath, reading, story telling, bottlefeeding (or for older kids, glasses of water), or anything else that involves a routine of some kind that your child will grow to expect. Before bed is a special time for mothers and their children, especially if you are a working mom and don't feel like you're spending enough quality time with your child. Use the daily tasks as times to be close to your child. Also, children thrive on routine and will be more likely to go to sleep peacefully once they've done the same things night after night and understand that after they've finished the routine, it's time for them to go to sleep.

When the baby is a newborn, let her sleep where there is lots of activity during the day and in a quiet environment at night so that she learns the difference between night and day quickly. We let our daughter sleep in the living room during the day (in a swing, the car seat, on the floor), and she went into her bed only at night. During night feedings, the lights were off, and nobody talked. She slept through the night at eight weeks.

Do you have pets? Do you have a child afraid of monsters in the dark? A great way to alleviate fears is to tell your kids that monsters are afraid of your family cat or dog, or even lizards. Suddenly, little ones relax and know as long as good old Rusty is there, nothing will happen to them.

My daughter is eleven months old now and just got through another phase of waking often during the night. She was waking up one or two hours before her usual time. I just fed her then put her back down to sleep or got up and had an early or extra-long nap time. It was probably a growth spurt, especially if food was the only thing that sent her back to sleep. It was a little rough on me, but it only lasted two or three weeks. It could be caused by her teeth, too, but if she goes back to sleep without taking any medication for teething, I lean toward the growth spurt thing.

My pediatrician told me that babies over six months old no longer need a middle-of-the-night feeding, but my baby was still waking up each night for a bottle out of habit. Here's how I got him to sleep through the night. I phased out the feedings so gradually he hardly noticed the changes. The first night, instead of his usual four ounces of formula, I gave him only three. I continued that for a few nights. The next change was to go to two ounces. I kept that up a few days before reducing the amount again, to one ounce, and finally to a bottle that had little more than a few sips. I made sure whenever I came into the baby's room that the interruption of sleep would be as short as possible. I never warmed the bottle.

I never turned on the light, and I kept as quiet as possible while feeding the baby. If he stopped sucking at any point, I figured the feeding was over and put him right back in his crib. After a few nights of bottle sipping that lasted no more than a minute or two, my baby seemed ready to go the full night, so I decided to see what would happen if he cried upon waking, and I showed up but didn't give him a bottle. All I did when I went in was to pick him up for a brief cuddle then put him back down. He went right back to sleep. I did this for a few nights, and then one night — to my delight and amazement — he didn't cry at all but slept the whole night.

Not sleeping through the night until children are three or four years of age is normal and healthy behavior. Your children are not being difficult or manipulative; they are behaving in ways that are appropriate. Once you understand these simple truths, it becomes much easier to deal with parenting your child at night. Once you give up the idea that you must have eight hours of uninterrupted sleep at night and view these nighttime interactions with your child as precious and fleeting, you get used to them very quickly.

Nighttime interactions with your child are precious, but you get used to them very quickly. I agree with the part about giving up the idea that you must have eight hours of uninterrupted sleep at night. I see so many people griping, "Yeah, but I work" and so forth, or, "I'm a zombie," but I very much believe it's mind over matter. When you believe that what's right for your children matters more than anything—and when you believe (which is tough!) that *you can cope with it* till you get used to it—you can do it!

⤚◉⤙

I am a mother of two. I have a three-year-old son and a one-year-old daughter. My husband and I plan on having two more children. My advice would be to relish their childhood because all too soon they're strong-willed teenagers, then ever-so-independent adults.

⤚◉⤙

I have a tape I play at bedtime and even at nap times. My girls are so used to the sound of this tape (and yes, we've made backups!) that they're like Pavlov's dogs. A few notes and they're sleepy! Bedtime is a twenty-minute breeze: brush teeth, read a few stories, pop the tape in, and we're outta there!

⤚◉⤙

On bedtime: While your infant is tiny, invest in a lullaby tape. We have one that has the sounds of a heartbeat in the background. We play it every night.

⤚◉⤙

On sleeping, do not do anything once that you don't want to continue for a lifetime — rocking to sleep, nursing to sleep, giving water, reading stories. Start at four months putting the baby down for naps when he's still awake. If he cries, come back in two minutes and stroke his back, talk softly, and leave. Come back in five minutes if the baby is still crying and go through the same procedure. As long as you know the baby is not sick, hungry, or wet, continue this until he is asleep. When he knows you are not going to cuddle and let him out of his bed, he will eventually learn that bed is a sleeping place.

All of our children have had their bouts of nighttime fright. Monsters under the bed, shadows on the wall — the dark can conjure up all kinds of fears. My husband and I decided to give them flashlights so if they see scary things on the wall or near the door, all they have to do is turn the flashlight on and scare all the bad guys away. Now they are no longer afraid, and we get some sleep. A little light can feel like a powerful thing.

Fooling children into going to sleep can really be a challenge sometimes. One tactic I use is a special concoction I like to call "sleepy-time powder." I told my children that it is a magic powder created by fairies to help little ones sleep. It's basically just baby powder with glitter thrown in. When it's bedtime, but the kids are bent on staying awake, I sprinkle a tiny bit around their room and tell them the magic will put them to sleep. After that, nothing can keep them awake! This potion also seems to work well as a way to monster-proof the bedroom (as long as you change the color of the glitter).

I have a daughter who has always had trouble with the dark. Even the night light doesn't always work. She's just so afraid of the closet monster. I have a few tricks that work pretty well. Sometimes we sing a monster song together to ward off any monsters that might dare come into her room. Other times I give her a necklace of mine that makes noise when you shake it. It makes her feel like she's driving the monsters away when she shakes it around her bed and the closet.

Our bedtime routine for our two-year-old consists of both playtime and winding-down time. Though she's frequently sleepy and cranky around dinnertime, and we think she might be ready for bed, she tends to get a second wind and be full of energy later on. So we try to get her to burn up that excess energy by playing chasing games, horsey, and other physical activities with her. After ten or twenty minutes of running around, she's ready to have a warm bath, get into her p.j.'s, brush her teeth, and listen to a story in her bed. By 8:00 P.M. she's lying down, and by 8:15, she's almost always fast asleep.

⁓⦿⦿

Tempting though it may be to rock your baby to sleep at nap time or bedtime—don't. The baby will soon become so used to this soothing service that he'll become unable to go to sleep on his own. With our firstborn it took us a long, long time to be able to get him to go to sleep in his crib. With our second one, right from the start we would put him down in his crib when it was time, when he was tired but not yet asleep, and we'd turn off the lights, whisper, "Sleep tight," and gently close the door behind us. He quickly learned that this routine meant "sleep," and he only rarely cried after the door was closed.

⁓⦿⦿

Our children would drive us crazy at bedtime by asking for one last snack or glass of milk. We realized that unless we had some kind of a firm rule, "bedtime" would quickly become a meaningless term, so now we always ask them, right before they start brushing their teeth, "Are you sure you don't want anything else to eat or drink?" If the answer is no, then they brush their teeth and get right into bed, because the rule in our house is, "Nothing comes between toothbrush time and bedtime."

⁓⦿⦿

For your own sanity, establish a bedtime ritual early on and stick to it. At our house it's get into pajamas, brush teeth, and then Daddy (or Mommy) will read you *one* story. Then it's a hug and a kiss, and after that, you can have one and only one "callback." This can be a request for water or another hug and kiss, an escort to the bathroom, or another tucking in, but after that, we're done for the night. The only exceptions are for sickness or some other sort of emergency. Our children understand the ritual and know they can't whine or wheedle their way around it, no matter what clever tricks they try.

Bedtime depends on your lifestyle and your kids. At our house, we tend to let our six-year-old and three-year-old stay up fairly late — mostly because we do not want to see their bright shiny faces at 5:30 A.M. — which is what was happening when they went to bed at a "normal" time like 7:30 or 8:00 P.M. It works a whole lot better for us if they stay asleep while we have our morning showers and get ready for work (i.e., I actually get to eat my breakfast and maybe even have coffee and read the headlines). Neither kid seems to need huge amounts of sleep. Next year, both of them will be in school in the morning. Then we will adjust bedtime to make sure they get adequate rest and can get up on time to get ready for school. I heard a good suggestion for older kids. At one mom's house, kids have to be in their rooms by a certain time but not necessarily with the lights out. They can play quietly, read, or do homework, but they have to stay in there so the adults get some time to themselves. Seems like a good compromise.

I no longer have a "bedtime" for my daughter. The rule is that as long as she gets herself up in the morning and off to school on time and is reasonably cheerful about it, she can go to bed when she wants. This works for her. When we first started this, she stayed up all night once or twice but learned she really can't do that. She sometimes goes to bed right after supper (and occasionally before!) but usually stays up till about 10 or 11 P.M. on school nights.

Every mother has a hard time getting her child to sleep at night, but I found a foolproof way to get mine to sleep that has an added benefit. I tell my daughter, who is ten years old, that she can stay up as long as she wants if she is reading in bed. I found that she started to love reading and that she would soon fall asleep on her own. That's the best kind of solution to a problem: one in which both mom and child win!

My husband frequently travels on business. Something he and my daughter do together every night is read at bedtime. In order for her not to feel abandoned by her dad, I started buying her books and told her that her father wanted me to tell her this special story because he couldn't be there himself to tell it to her. She still misses him when he goes away, but she feels like he's there with her anyway and thinking about her because he didn't forget their special time together.

Bedwetting

All the males on my father's side of my family wet the bed when they slept. In my father's generation, they did it into adulthood. So it's clearly something genetic, and I suspect related to sleep patterns — all these guys are naturally *very* deep sleepers. Anyhow, now my three sisters and I all have bed-wetting sons. Mine was quick to toilet train at two and one half but still has no control while sleeping at night or during long daytime naps. I use large-sized diapers for him at night (he's five and weighs about forty-three pounds). My sister's older son is seven and was starting to get embarrassed about this — her pediatrician gave her an apparatus that buzzed when the boy wet the bed, thus waking him up. After several weeks of this, he learned to wake up consciously. That's what I plan to use, too. According to my pediatrician, if the apparatus doesn't work, and the kid doesn't grow out of the problem at puberty, it can be controlled by medication.

We tried everything else, and this worked. There is a contraption with an alarm that is attached to the under-wear with Velcro, and the alarm sits right on the shoulder. I could hardly believe it. My son is ten, and it took four nights of this alarm going off and us getting up immedi-ately with him and taking him to the bathroom, whether he had to go anymore or not. After that he wet one or two more nights (just a little), and now he's been dry for five months. I think the difference in this alarm from other apparatuses is that it sounds as soon as any damp-ness is felt, as opposed to the child lying on it so that it takes longer for the urine to get to the pad. He can finally go to sleep-overs and camp!

CLOTHES AND DRESSING

Dressing your children can range from suiting them up in adorable holiday outfits or cute swimsuits to coping with unwieldy snowsuits and other wintertime horrors. It can also be one of the most time-consuming activities of the day, depending on how interested the little ones are in being dressed! Then, just when you think the worst years are over, teenagers come along, and there is a whole new set of problems. Here, moms share time-saving tips and their own stories of frustration.

Don't all babies hate snowsuits? It's an endless struggle to put their arms and legs inside—and then a struggle again to get the things off when they're back in the house. It took me too long to realize that it wasn't necessary. When they're really small, they're better off in a bunting that just zips over their whole body. When they're older, choose a fleecy, warm pair of pants, warm socks, mittens, and a down parka, and they're ready for the arctic blasts.

Here's a great trick for learning how to put on a coat that our older child learned in nursery school. Lay out the coat on the floor, with its back to the floor, upside down, at the child's feet (hood or collar of the coat touching the child's toes). The child bends down and puts her arms into the sleeves while flipping the coat over her head (the parent may help with this the first few times). Amazingly, the coat is on right side up!

I don't have to carry both a diaper bag and a pocketbook. Instead, I use a backpack for everything. I have a small-sized diaper pad that folds up and fits into an outer pocket of the backpack, but I have also seen specially designed backpacks in the Land's End catalog that come with their own matching diaper pads. The advantage to a backpack is that it's a hands-free bag, and it's gender-neutral, so dads don't mind taking it along when they're out with the baby.

I've found the most convenient way to carry my baby supplies is in a fanny-pack. It's so simple just to grab it and snap it around my waist whenever I'm about to take the baby somewhere. It's not terribly big so I've had to learn to be very efficient about packing it up — but that's helped me to be better organized.

To encourage little girls to learn to dress themselves, don't buy any complicated blouses, jumpers, or button-in-back dresses. Let them wear leggings instead of tights. Stick to one-piece, over-the-head, loose, cotton dresses, or t-shirts and elastic-waist pants. Unless you want to spend several minutes every morning tying their shoes (until about age six), buy only shoes that close with Velcro, slip-ons, or buckle shoes that have large, easy-to-see holes in the straps.

Our girls have frequently formed intense attachments to certain t-shirts or dresses. Even after they've outgrown the clothes, or the clothes have become hopelessly worn out, they beg me not to throw them away. I used to just hang on to them until my mom came up with a brilliant idea for keeping the clothes and getting some use from them at the same time. She showed me how to turn the old clothes into a quilt. She cut out large patches from the centers of the t-shirts and dresses to form a small patchwork design. Now my kids can have their old clothes forever, and we have a very nice story to tell whenever visitors ask us where we found that unusual quilt.

COMMUNICATION

Communication is a crucial element in raising children. Of all the rules of family, asking that members communicate with each other is the most helpful to the family unit and the best way to raise children who can connect with the world. It can also be the most undervalued and misunderstood aspect of family life. In this section, mothers share their ideas on how to interact with their children and how to get their sometimes-uncommunicative offspring to respond.

A New Baby

I'm always amazed at how intuitive my little daughter is. I'm pregnant with our second child, and my first is very aware of what's going on. She knows there is a big change happening with Mommy and the whole family. It's funny how much kids understand and pick up from their environment. Be careful with children during this delicate time. Make sure you communicate with them. Tell them how much you love them and explain what is going on so the birth won't be such a shock. Try to really involve them in the pregnancy as much as you can. Also, if the family is doing something special for the new arrival, make sure to do something special for the others, too. Arrange an activity that centers around them. Don't forget to keep it up after the baby is born, so they know you will always have time for them.

When you have a newborn baby, it's easy to fall into the habit of calling her "the baby." Try not to do this, though, because I've seen some moms who continue calling their child "the baby" for years and years!

When I was pregnant with my second child and my son was still a toddler, I was concerned that he would feel jealous about the new baby. I told him that his younger brother or sister would need him to watch out for him, protect him, and love him. I said that the new baby would love him as much as I did and that he would know it when the baby came home and squeezed his hand. When it came time for my new daughter to come home from the hospital, she wrapped her little fingers around my son's finger, and he fell in love! Now he can't do enough for her, and he doesn't feel jealous, only protective, of his little sister.

When you bring home a newborn, you might think, "I'm never going to get the hang of this." But don't despair! You will start to feel more comfortable with your skills and will figure out what works for you and your new family. Don't think that you're alone. Many resources are available to you. It helps to talk to other new moms to get ideas about what to do about various problems. What works for one baby or household may not necessarily work at your house, so gather lots of ideas and options to try out. Talking to other new moms is also a real sanity-saver—it will get you out of the house and seeing other adults. Many hospitals and community centers offer programs (i.e., new moms' discussion groups, parenting classes, and drop in centers). Trust me—they can really, really help. If nothing else, you will find out that others are going through the same thing, and you are not alone.

My midwife gave me a tip to figure out if my daughter was really hungry or if she was fussing for other reasons. Touch the baby's cheek with a finger. A hungry child will turn her head and suck the finger. A nonhungry child won't. I imagine this only works for tiny babies, but I found it helpful.

Baby monitors are fine for letting you know when your baby has woken up from a nap, but as she gets older, you'll find it's much more useful to have a two-way device that lets you talk to your toddler or answer her request for a late-night drink of water by saying, "Okay, but you'll have to wait a few minutes." We've found that a room-to-room intercom will provide the monitoring capability of the traditional baby monitor, but parents of older toddlers will appreciate the ability to talk back.

If you're divorcing, explain that your whole family won't be living together anymore, but that the child will have as few changes in her life as possible. Be honest about what is going on, but don't mention information that would demean the other parent. As hard as it is, don't submit a child to your own insecurities and unhappiness. Nothing hurts worse than to see your child depressed and unhappy and know that you've added to it. Don't tell the child that your lack of money or things has to do with the other parent. After your child sees the other parent, don't ask questions about money, his dates, or anything that would force your child to take sides. Even if the other parent belittles you in front of the child, at least your child has a safe haven with you.

If you are a divorced parent, I would suggest giving loads of hugs and kisses and trying to spend plenty of time with your kids, but don't feel like you need to buy or do special things to make up for the situation. They just want to know that they are loved, secure, and safe.

To avoid jealousy between little ones, make sure to set aside the appropriate amount of time for everyone. Don't keep interrupting time you're spending with one sibling for another. It breeds anger and frustration. Also, encourage each child's special talents. If you cultivate a separate and distinct talent in each child, they won't feel the need to compete with one another as much.

Talk to your baby, beginning at birth. Don't assume that your baby cannot understand you—you'd be surprised at what a baby comprehends. Describe everywhere you go and everything you do. Talk to everyone you meet and include your baby in the conversation. Whatever you do, don't use baby words—your baby will just have to unlearn them later.

My little one had a habit of calling herself "stupid" for any tiny infraction. This can be dangerous, so be careful. You don't want their self-esteem to be damaged. Have them tell you a few good things about themselves, a few things they like. Don't let them put themselves down and never call them names yourself. As parents, our job is to build their self-esteem, not tear it down.

If you aren't sure exactly what it is that a child is painting, don't say, "That's beautiful. What is it?" These comments tend to hurt feelings. How could mom not know? The best thing to do is get him to talk about it. Ask him to tell you all about the picture. This way, he will be thrilled that you are so interested, and you will have a tiny window into your child's mind. What is he thinking when he paints? How did he come up with the idea?

I like books that have a lot going on on each page so there's lots to look at and discuss. Like how to build a wooden house (ours is made from twenty-inch-thick stone walls), why the postman in some places both brings and collects outgoing mail (here the postman delivers individual mail but collects from communal post boxes), why a house is built before the occupants move in (here most houses are sold by prior occupants to new owners), why none of the road signs pictured is used here, why the gas station attendant fills up your car or someone washes it for you, just what is a "busboy," and so on.

I found that some books intended for adults that use lots of pictures to explain how things work were useful when my daughter was five and six, even though they were quite a ways beyond her reading ability; the pictures were enormously informative, and I like to think that supplying her with books that were too hard for her to read was part of what inspired her to become such an avid reader.

DISCIPLINE AND GUIDANCE

No parent has the answer to the problem of disciplining children, and more than a few theories are floating around. Should we spank children? Should we raise our voices? Will whatever method we use do any good at all? There is only one thing every family can agree on: The act of disciplining changes from family to family, and different methods work for different kids.

I discovered a great technique for potty training while I was raising my children. Try letting your children run around without a diaper on. The feeling acts as a reminder not to go to the bathroom. It works great and is just as useful for girls as for boys.

Our two daughters — ages three and five — like to get up early on weekend mornings, and I like to sleep in after a long week at work. Because they're old enough to entertain themselves without me, I make a ritual the night before by helping them select a "morning toy" that they can play with to keep them occupied. Sometimes it's just a stuffed animal or a book that I will leave on their nightstands, but it will give me an extra half hour or so of sleep so I can be fully rested to spend a long day with them.

My two boys love to tattle on each other, so I've devised a neat trick to put an end to it as soon as it starts. I tell them we're playing a game and that the first time one of them says the other's name, he loses. That stops the "Mommy, Joey did . . ." or "Billy won't . . ." right away!

I have twin eight-year-old daughters who always feel like they're in competition for my time and attention. So once a month they have a day of their own. On "Mommy days"—usually Saturday—I spend the whole day with one of my daughters, leaving the other with my husband. She is free to have us do whatever she wants: shopping, going to the movies, walking in the park, whatever. This time together helps to eliminate some of their feelings of competition, and I find that it also gives us precious quality time in which I can learn more about their lives.

Strong limit-setting is imperative, but avoid saying "no." If you develop the discipline necessary to avoid this, you also develop a wide repertoire of positive parenting techniques. The word "no" will retain its power if it is used only in situations where safety is involved or when there is no room for equivocation. I am a parent of two sons and have been a preschool teacher for more than twenty years. Few things are as sad as a parent who shrilly proclaims, "No!" only to be ignored by his child. Once you lose your credibility with your child, it is difficult to regain. I used the word "taboo" in place of "no." It was difficult to say it without retaining my sense of humor, and it was also hard to say with anger in my voice. Over time, however, it became extremely effective. If a mother avoids saying "no," she is forced to develop effective alternatives. Anything that requires one to actually be conscious while parenting can only help children and parents.

Sometimes when my husband and I give too much attention to our other children or the new baby, our toddler throws a tantrum. This seems to be the only time, though. Whenever it happens, one of us takes him into the other room and talks to him or plays with him. We are trying to show him that we haven't forgotten about him and that we are still interested in what he is doing.

Other times our son just wants to say "no" and get angry. We try a variety of things in a scenario such as this. First we take a time out; then, if that doesn't work, we send him to his room. These old standbys seem to work pretty well.

Here are some suggestions for getting a child to practice—anything—although here I'll concentrate on practicing piano. These suggestions are most appropriate for ages two through seven:

• Remember the real purpose of learning music at a very young age, which should be to engender a love of music. You can't do that if you make it drudgery for the child.

• The best way to learn to love music and to play music is to listen to *good* music. Your child should have music playing in the background as much as possible.

• Make up different practicing games. Use sticker charts and dice to assign various songs that need practicing. Have your child throw the dice. Whatever number comes up, the child plays the corresponding song. Have little animals or tiny erasers that the child can pick out of a bag and line up on the piano every time she plays a song or, if she's just learning the song, a measure or two. Stage performances when you have your child line up her stuffed animals to be the audience. Or make dates for a special performance when the family sits down to listen to a "real" concert by the child. Don't make it lonely: This is the hardest thing for busy parents, but children at this age do not like to do these things by themselves. At least one parent or caregiver needs to spend practice time with the child.

• Take your cues from your child. I've found that the best time to practice is after breakfast, before my child goes to school. She is too tired after school, and when a child starts to have homework, after-school time will be taken up with that. When you see your child getting tired or too challenged by a particular practice session, change what he is doing . . . again, if possible, with a game. Instead of making a child play a piece that is hard, let her pick one she wants to play. Or work on sight reading or theory in ways that are fun for children. Or end the session for the day. No one should be forced to play when she's tired. There's always tomorrow.

• Make sure you set aside a specific time each day for practicing. Children like to know what to expect and what is expected of them. Although children may resist practicing, if they get used to a schedule it will soon become just another part of their day.

• Remember, don't expect your children to progress according to your own desires. They have their own internal clocks and natural desires to learn and please. If you make it fun, they will want to play.

When it comes to avoiding temper tantrums, I follow the three basic rules. The time rule: Announce the time before changing anything. Tell little Jimmy he has five minutes until it is time to go. Announce when it will happen often. This reminds him to prepare for an activity change. It also helps him begin to set mental schedules. The second tactic I use is carrying a distracting item into the new activity. I bring games, toys, or anything else (sometimes his blankie) to a new event. Blankie comes with us for particularly stressful events. The third trick I use is to try to keep life regimented. I don't like to leave too much up in the air. A lack of boundaries doesn't work well for children. They need a carefully planned routine so they know what's coming next and they feel a structure in their lives.

I'm not sure what the story is, but my child is fairly tantrum-free. In fact, I remember my mother telling me I was the same way. The worst I get is a few "going limp" episodes. But that only seems to happen when we're shopping, and I've kept my little one out too long. I think my good luck has come from being predictable and consistent. My mother was the same way. If you give children a routine, something to count on, they will really respond to it.

My daughter is a lot like I was when I was little. She is so afraid to speak up for herself. She is fine with her playmates and friends. But when she has an abrasive teacher or other children pick on her, she becomes withdrawn and nonconfrontational. It isn't that I want her to be a bully, but she can't stand up for herself verbally. The worst is that her self-esteem seems to be suffering. She gets so angry at herself and calls herself a wimp. I have spoken up for her in the past, but it seems to make matters worse. Then she feels like Mom is coming to the rescue again. The best way (so far) to work out a compromise in these sensitive situations is to tell my daughter I will be with her when she has to speak up for herself (to a teacher or doctor, for example), but I will not do the talking for her. This helps her to get up the courage to confront her fears.

Isn't every parent nervous about having the "birds-and-bees" talk? When that fateful day arrives, be prepared. I wanted to make sure I was. When my daughter started school, I asked her teachers if and when they were going to have a sex-ed course. Good thing I asked, because fifth grade was when the course started. I wanted to beat them to the punch, so I started talking to my girl right away. I'm glad I did. Just that week, I found a book shoved under her mattress that was all about teen problems like sex and depression. I was shocked. If I had known she needed to talk about these problems or even was thinking about them, I would have started earlier. Don't wait too long. Apparently, kids start to learn and wonder way earlier than I thought. By the time they are twelve or so, they don't want to talk about anything. True to form, they think they know everything, and you couldn't possibly understand. At least if you communicate with them early, they know you are there for them, and they can come to you when they need to.

One mother shared insights that she acquired through raising an only child:

Be careful around the gender areas! A little joke, but it's true. If a mother is trying to raise a son, she needs to understand that she *doesn't* understand what the son is going through at puberty, with hormones and all that. Also, remember that the son *does not* want to discuss it with his mother. Only a father or father figure is qualified in the child's mind to discuss what he is going through.

The mother needs to try to keep her period under control around a boy! Before the boy is smart enough to realize and understand PMS and that *special* time of the month, he'll think that his mother is a monster once a month. Even after he understands, the mother should be up front with her son (to a point) so that there won't be any confusion about her gender. Emotionally stability is low in young boys, so it is partly the mothers' duty to instill it.

─◆─

Basically, parents shouldn't be afraid to say "no." I have found that often parents overcompensate for their busy work schedules, divorces, limited child-visitation time, or whatever by giving their son or daughter *anything* the child desires. I know, I've been there. When I was going through a rough divorce, I bought and bought and bought for my young daughter. Later, I financed her way through *five* colleges and a lifestyle that included semesters at colleges in Boca Raton, Florida, and San Diego, California. Today, after I cut off this aid, she is financing her own college degree (she graduated in December 1997) and is getting straight A's and B's at a private Catholic women's college. Kids need boundaries.

My daughter told me she wished I had been tougher with chore assignments and helping in the kitchen, as it would have been easier for her when she got her own apartment.

~

My advice is: Don't sweat the little stuff. In other words, the big issues, such as respect for parents, curfews, not doing dangerous or illegal things (like drinking or smoking), we make a big deal of. The little things, like what the kids want to wear (as long as they don't offend), hairstyles, make-up, bedtimes, don't sweat. Another suggestion: Negotiate. Teach a child how to argue his points. You have your vantage point, he has his. Meeting somewhere in the middle will make both happy. Otherwise, the child will learn manipulation, and the adult will continue to use preemptive power, which will be the lesson passed on. Here is an example: When the child is little, bedtimes are a problem. Let him help decide his own bedtime, and if he continues to dawdle, ask him to set a time limit for himself as to when he will go to bed. Will he go to bed in ten minutes or five? Does he want his teddy bear or another toy? (This is negotiation, which doesn't always mean haggling.) Be firm once a decision is made, but stay flexible.

Toilet Training

When potty training, we found it made sense to bypass the potty-on-the-floor stage and go right to the big toilet. We got one of those seats you put over the adult seat that made it very inviting for a small child to sit down and put a step stool in front of the toilet so that she could get on and off by herself. We are careful not to flush while she's sitting there because she doesn't like the noise. It's really great not to have to clean out any dirty potties.

For our son to get the idea of toilet training, he had to be able to feel when he had gone in his pants. Disposable diapers and Pull-Ups are so absorbent that he never was sure if he was wet. On the other hand, I didn't want to put him straight into underwear and have to wash it all the time. Since summer was near, and he'd be spending much of the day outside, I decided the thing to do was to let him run around naked as much as possible. We moved his potty outdoors whenever he went out and kept it in whatever room he was playing while inside. Within a few days, he was pretty dependable.

Remember the idea of potty training boys by giving them something to aim at? Like Cheerios? Well, that basic idea can be altered in lots of fun ways. For a change, try soap in the potty. Boys get a big kick out of making bubbles.

When potty training isn't going well from the start, the thing to do is to stop making a battle out of it. Put the child back in diapers for at least two or three weeks and maybe even a month or two. Wait till your child brings up the idea of using the potty on her own, or you could bring up the subject yourself, but wait until the child seems more receptive to the process. The promise of some sort of reward for each day spent in clean, dry underwear may help the child to want to achieve the goal.

The secret to successful toilet training is finding the right incentive for your particular child. For some children, it's the idea of being a big boy or big girl and getting to wear underwear just like daddy or mommy. For those children, Pull-Ups are probably a mistake. For other children, rewards for each successful use of the potty will work well. In the case of my own daughter, it was the promise of getting to wear a sequined skirt. I told her it wouldn't fit well over a diaper, and it might be ruined forever if she had an accident in it, so she had to be extraspecial careful to remember to go to the potty when she was wearing it. She wore it for several weeks on end and never once had an accident with it on.

My son (age three years and eight months) has steadfastly refused potty training. It is something we have discussed, something he has tried, something he knows he is capable of doing, but something he for some reason is not yet ready to do full time. That is what my son is announcing, and we are reinforcing his decision and counting on his sticking to it. Our theory? Kids develop at different rates in different areas, and this is simply one area where our son is developing more slowly. And that should be perfectly acceptable.

The one lesson I learned while trying to potty train my two-year-old daughter is to make it fun! If you can make a game out of what is usually a chore, the little ones learn faster. Now, when it's potty time, we play special games that are reserved only for that time. My daughter isn't fidgety, and she has something fun to do while she's in the bathroom.

Once your child is of school age and can read numbers, get him a digital alarm clock. Set the clock for whatever time the child needs to be up in the morning. Lay out school clothes for him the night before and make him responsible for getting up at the alarm, dressing himself, brushing his own teeth, and coming downstairs in time to have breakfast and board the school bus or carpool on time. If you can get your child adjusted to these responsibilities from kindergarten or first grade on, you'll avoid years of nagging and fighting later on.

Throwing Tantrums

It is important to distinguish between tantrum types. There are two. One is a tantrum thrown due to exhaustion or frustration, and the other is a tantrum caused by not getting what you want. If there is a legitimate reason for a tantrum such as being too tired, the reaction makes sense. No child can have the stamina of an adult. I am fully sympathetic to this and usually end up apologizing about pushing them too hard. However, if it is a tantrum due to selfishness or acting spoiled, there is no way I am going to respond or give in. I have never humored that kind of tantrum. I think that is why we have so few now. I have actually told my children that a tantrum will not help them get what they want.

When children throw tantrums in public, try these techniques. Tell them it is not all right for them to act that way. Explain. Give them the benefit of the doubt. Sometimes telling them what will happen gives children a perspective they didn't have before. Say to them, "When you do this, you make Mommy feel bad. How can Mommy help make you feel better?" That type of language. If they continue or are abusive (telling you they don't care if you're upset), then tell them you will both have to leave. Don't let the misbehavior continue. Keep the promise and leave. Try going home or somewhere private and not very fun. Make sure to follow through with the threat. Then explain what you have done. Tell your child, "We left because you are not allowed to act that way in public. Because you misbehaved, we had to go home." Then, hopefully, the child will make the connection and remember it next time. I know this is a big pain, but it is very effective.

❦

Overall, my daughter is pretty well behaved. She did go through a tantrum phase, which I guess all kids do, when she was around seventeen or eighteen months old. I had heard about a technique where you hold and soothe your child rather than trying to discipline them with force. I thought that would work better because of the kind of tantrums she had. They weren't "I want that, you're not letting me have it" types of tantrums, they were more out of frustration. I tried it, and it really seemed to work, at least with my girl. I think children go through a lot parents don't understand. They have a lot of frustrating things happening in their lives. They are absorbing and learning more every day, and sometimes it can be hard, especially when they are trying to voice their feelings or explain something, and they can't quite get it out. It gets confused and jumbled in their heads, and little ones get mad. This is totally understandable.

I have tried to be gentle and soothing during tantrums, but with my girl, it just doesn't work. If it does anything at all, it makes her more upset. It's almost like she just has to get it out of her system, and if I get in the way — forget it. It only gets worse, and her frenzy gets more violent. Usually she gets it out and by the end has forgotten why she was so upset in the first place. In this type of situation, I've found it works better to ignore her, so she can work it out alone. I feel awful doing this. It is really difficult for me to ignore her, but I know it is the only thing I can do.

I don't know why exactly, but I have never had a tantrum problem with my children. They have never thrown tantrums. I've seen it before, in the mall or the grocery store, but I've never experienced it. I was asking my own mother about my sister and me, and she said we never had tantrums either. In fact, we never had a problem going to bed, taking a bath, any of that. I remember that, too. I think kids are different, and different tactics work for each individual child. My mother, however, believes it is all in the parenting. If you don't communicate with children, then they will reward you with many tantrums. She told me that she would simply explain *why* I had to go to the doctor or not have the toy, I would understand, and that would be the end of it. I remember that, too. Whenever Mom or Dad explained, it made sense, and I was fine.

For some reason, giving my children more choices seems to keep tantrums away. Usually, I've heard, it works the other way around. Most of my friends say that more boundaries are the key. But I think, with my child, because life is so out of her control, any little bit of control on her part is very helpful. In a way she feels like she is participating in her own upbringing!

My child has tantrums. Boy, does she. I cannot deal with it at all. I have so little patience for this sort of thing. Usually, I just sit a few yards away and ride it out. Most people walk by and give me terrible looks, but what else can I do? People are always going to look at you and think bad things because they either don't have children or their kids don't have tantrums. I hate it when other adults get involved. I think to myself, "Like you know anything about what I'm going through. When you have children, then look at me like that." They always think you're being mean. Weren't any of these people children themselves? I know for a fact that there are quite a few adults who act like children, and the same tactics work on them. Don't they realize that, or do they live in a world where no one is unreasonable?

Try this when your child is screaming or having a tantrum: Whisper or speak in a very soft voice. Make sure the child can see you so that he knows you're talking to him. He'll probably stop screaming in order to hear what you are saying.

On Giving Up the Blankie

Blankies are forever. At least in bed. I slept with my blankie in or on my bed for years. My brother carried his blankie around so much that it started falling apart. My mom cut it into strips, and he carried a piece of his blankie with him in his pocket for a long time. I don't see any need to remove comfort items. At twelve years of age my son still sleeps with a bed full of stuffed animals. Only a couple of them are treasured, the rest just live there. His chimpanzee went with him to both church and scout camps this past summer.

We finally took the bottle away from my daughter at about two. By that time, she was down to one on most days anyway, but the real motivation was to end the constant criticism by a certain relative. She was upset for a few days but then started sucking on other things — clothes, toys — for a few months. In retrospect, I wish I had just let her decide when she wanted to give it up, especially since we only allowed water in bottles.

I know from my pediatrician, who was just appalled, that putting off weaning from his bottle is not the currently approved method. I did not see, though, that my son's attachment to the bottle did him any harm, then or now. His teeth are straight, no cavities (we didn't let him sleep with a bottle of anything but plain water, and we brush his teeth mornings and evenings). The bottle was an indispensable comfort tool during those emotionally volatile twos and threes, and it didn't spill, unlike even a well-designed sippy cup.

I went cold turkey with my son. We went on vacation, and when we came home, the bottle fairy had been there, and all of the bottles were gone! Kind of like the tooth fairy, only we didn't put the bottles under his pillow before we left. For the life of me, I can't remember how old he was when I did this.

~•~

Well, now that I actually think about it, I guess a good bit of advice is that children know nothing of the concept of quality time. Any time you spend with them is a tremendous gift to them and yourself. If you relegate it to a certain finite amount each day, you lose something precious.

~•~

Our son was a problem biter and hair-puller at about eighteen months. He was big for his age, which exacerbated the situation because he was able to do more damage than the average eighteen-month-old. We worked together with his daycare on this. We asked his teacher to keep a log of problems during the day; we kept a similar log at home for nights and weekends. After two weeks we compared notes and found that the incidents were occurring at predictable times—right before lunch and right after dinner. Increasing his physical activity at those times (at daycare, they sent him outside with slightly older children) had a dramatic effect; we saw virtually no biting or hair-pulling once we changed his routine. The daycare was so impressed with the results that they modified the teachers' log, and it is now part of regular teacher training.

Our son still (at almost five) occasionally bites as a sort of reflex to being startled or overexcited. Each time, we are very clear that it hurts, and if it happens during a fun time (like wrestling on the floor or something), we stop the fun right away so he gets the clear message that biting hurts and the fun stops.

When there is just one cookie left in the jar, and there are two children who want it, here is a solution worthy of King Solomon: One child gets to divide the cookie in half. The other child gets to choose which half he wants.

Our son had to learn the hard way never to pet a strange dog. Even if it looks friendly and is on a leash, a dog can react unpredictably to a small child's approach. It may snarl or even bite. Make sure you keep small children away from all unleashed dogs, and if the dog is on a leash with its owner, get the owner's okay before you let your child move within the dog's range.

If you notice that your baby is developing an attachment to a special stuffed animal or blanket, buy a duplicate before the original becomes worn or discolored. If you let a teddy get old and frayed and then you misplace it, your child will be devastated and will not accept a substitute because it will look too different. But if you have two of the same security object, and you let both get used and worn at about the same rate, the child will consider them interchangeable. To be even safer, if you can get three or four of the loved object, you'll never have to worry about losing one.

We taught our children from a young age to understand about how long ten minutes was, and five minutes, and one minute. Whenever they had to leave a playground or a friend's house, they'd first hear, "Ten more minutes," then "five minutes," and then "one minute." When it was time to leave, they understood there would be no more delays—that was it. These regular announcements about time have also helped to establish a set bedtime. They know when they're down to the one-minute warning that their teeth have to be brushed and their pajamas on, because time is almost up.

If you want to "pay" your child a "salary," at fourteen she could be given enough to start making budgets. For example, provide enough to pay for school lunches and clothing as well as the occasional compact disk and candy (which I hope is the worst thing your child wants to ingest!), and let her figure out how much she can spend from week to week on what things.

This is what my mom did for me regarding allowance; I think I was around fifteen. She picked an amount based on what she thought was reasonable, we discussed it and agreed on it, and that was my money for the month for clothes, outings, and the like. It worked out really well, I thought — I learned to make my own decisions about whether I'd rather buy these shoes or that CD — and made me realize just how expensive certain things were.

I've based my parenting style on techniques I learned while working with developmentally disabled children. My basic philosophy is to harp on the positive. I try to reinforce all positive behavior in my two children (ages three and five) by telling them constantly what a good job they're doing. I do this in many ways: by simply telling them, by hugging them and telling them, by smiling, by thanking them, or by saying how proud I am of them. Friends of mine occasionally say, "It doesn't work with my child. He doesn't care about that." But my belief is that there is no child (or grown-up, for that matter) out there who does not like to hear good things about himself. Perhaps it won't work for the moment in getting them to do what the parent wants at that time, but over time it will have an impact — a positive one. There will always be times when I am not "proud" of my child's behavior, but I think the number of those times has been minimized by "accentuating the positive."

I might be considered too lax in my method, but I handled the use of bad language by suggesting expletives that I didn't mind so much, like crap, crud, rats, shoot. I told my boys that if they just had to use worse language than that it must not be overheard by adults, girls, or children younger than them. I also gave them a list of the ones that I would *not* tolerate under any circumstances. I know this isn't going to solve the problem, and I let them know I didn't approve of *any* bad language, but it's all around us, and I can't seem to control all of the bad habits that they pick up.

When leaving a child at school, be honest and tell him when you will be back. Don't let the child know that you, too, are feeling anxious. Don't linger at the place you are dropping off. Drop off at the door and leave immediately. When you pick up, don't say, "It's okay, Mommy's here," as if it were not okay when you weren't. Say positive things: "What a great time you must have had."

Homework is for the child, not you. You may explain if they are stuck, but don't sit and go through each problem. If they are having that much trouble, set up a teacher conference and find out why they don't understand. Also, if it seems that they have too much homework converse with other parents and ask if their children have a lot of homework. Chances are the children have plenty of time to do it in class but have chosen not to, especially if they think, "Mom will be there to do it with me, and I'll get attention — positive or negative."

I think the most important thing to always keep in mind as a parent is that every child is different, whether it's your first and your second, or your sister's son and yours, or you and your own children. No one strategy works with every child the same way. The key is to know your kids and know what they will respond to. I have tried to do this by teaching my kids what to respond to. In the first three years of life, we as parents have a unique time window in which to shape our children's thought processes. In my situation, I raised two infants who were born before and during my time in law school. Time was of the essence, as you can imagine. I dealt with my kids by setting their schedules to coincide with mine. Both were sleeping through the night by three months. Also, the bottle was gone by the time they were a year old. However, my daughter had a pacifier until she was two. So you see, you win some and you lose some. But as with anything in life, you have to know what battles you need to win in order to win the war. By that, I mean know what is important to you, and let go a little on the not-so-important things.

When leaving a play area, I give my children plenty of prep time. I make sure I'm face to face and not shouting across the park or play area. I tell them they have five minutes, just enough time for three slides, or whatever. In two minutes I give them another warning and tell them what I expect of them: One more slide, then you have to come put your shoes back on. When that time limit is up, I praise them for remembering (even when they haven't, really), put the shoes on, and leave. On the way home I encourage them to share their feelings about the playtime. "I had a great time at the park. What about you kids?" We rarely have a scene when it's time to go; they just need some warning.

Discipline has to be consistent. Don't make threats that you don't follow through on. Don't use the phrase "the next time." Don't be afraid to discipline your child in public. You can always take him outside or to the bathroom to scold. Or for heaven's sake, go home or take away a privilege. I consider any outside activity like dance, baseball, or swimming a privilege.

Praise your child, praise him in public, let him hear you tell someone what a great job he did at whatever. Try to find something he's doing right, even if it's difficult to single something out. Like: Thank you so much for not picking your nose, you are really growing up to be such a terrific person. Send a special note in his lunch once in a while. Hug your children, love them, and try to talk to them as if you were talking to your best friend — with respect.

Start very young to teach children to love other things besides themselves, such as animals and friends. Teach them how to share. Teach them how to take care of their toys and belongings. Show them how to make a peanut butter sandwich at two years old and how to clean up the mess. Let them learn to do things for themselves, by themselves. Our purpose as parents is to raise responsible and caring citizens. If we always help, if we never say no, then we are not accomplishing that goal.

Sibling Disputes

Teach them the skills they need to solve the problem by showing them how to negotiate. Instead of letting them scream because someone wants a toy, have them consider offering a trade for it. "Sarah, I'll trade you this Mickey Mouse for your horsey?" Often this will work, keeping you out of the loop altogether.

Have you ever played the staring game when you were little? Well, the same premise seems to work when resolving fights. If you have bickering children, just tell them to stare at each other silently for a few minutes. Usually, one of them breaks a few seconds in, and there is an explosion of giggling. This works just as well between mom and dad, too!

Don't spend so much time reasoning with your children. It gives them a chance to try to change your mind or argue with you. Be direct and to the point. It is actually easier on children to have these limits. They need to know where the boundaries are. Simple commands let them know you mean business.

When disciplining a child, try to be positive and reinforcing. Encourage him with comments like, "Good job!" or, "Wow, you were really paying attention." They really get excited by the fuss, and they try harder to get that praise. Children have a real need to impress their parents. My parents did the same thing for me. When I would brush my teeth, they would put on their sunglasses and pretend my teeth were so shiny they could hardly see. It was fun for me, and I looked forward to brushing to get that positive feedback.

If two children want to do the same thing at the same time, tell them they must take turns. Then they'll both want to have the first turn, of course, so the next thing you say is, "The one who goes second will get a longer turn." This solution has usually satisfied both of my kids.

Try to avoid putting questions to toddlers in a form that gets a yes-or-no answer. Ninety-nine percent of the time, if you ask a two-year-old, "Do you want to put on your shoes now?" the answer will be, "No!" In fact, for a year and a half I thought the only word my two-year-old could say was no. Far better to put the shoe question like this: "It's time to put on your shoes now. You can choose your sneakers or your sandals." That way you have at least a hope of getting a cooperative answer.

Children will cooperate in cleaning up if you turn it into a game. Tell them to race you, and if they can get all the blocks picked up off the floor before you finish doing the dishes, they win. Let your older child and your younger child take turns clearing the table and putting the dishes in the dishwasher; one can be allowed to run the garbage disposal while the other one gets to fill the dishwasher detergent compartment and start the wash cycle.

I was afraid if I was constantly telling my child not to do this or that or criticizing her bad behavior that she might come to think of herself as a bad girl. So I invented a terrible brat named Ditsy who can never seem to do anything right. Whenever I want to teach my child not to do a particularly naughty or dangerous thing, I tell her what happened to Ditsy when she tried the same thing. Ditsy was always having tantrums and getting sent to her room, and even though her parents told her and told her what not to do, she never seemed to learn and was constantly in trouble. My daughter loved hearing these stories simply because it was fascinating to hear about someone who would do all of these forbidden activities, but she understood that Ditsy led a miserable life, and my daughter now makes a deliberate effort not to be like her.

Since part of our jobs as parents is to raise children who will have good table manners and are socially competent, that is, conforming to the customs and traditions of our society, my advice would be not to give in to your two-year-old's demands to eat dessert before the entrée. If she refuses to eat her dinner unless she eats dessert first, you could require her to sit with the family while they eat and then excuse her from the table while everyone else has dessert. At this point, she may change her mind and at least sample her entrée in order to have dessert. On the other hand, if she is strong-willed and more interested in control and power games, she may not. If she throws a tantrum, you can remove her from the eating area until the rest of the family can enjoy their meal in peace. A night or two of getting no dessert at all should change her behavior.

One of the ways that I have handled the really obnoxious attitudes my children give me is to just walk away. I don't correct (hey, they know they are being rude), I don't complain, I just leave. It lets them know that I respect myself too much to be treated that way. A lot of the time my daughter will come back to me with a whole different attitude.

One mother had a suggestion for integrating younger and older kids during an activity such as drawing:

You can't possibly keep all the writing tools out of a child's way with older kids around. He'll learn in a while and outgrow the wall-scribbling phase, but you can help that along. It will take a few days of vigilance on your part. Try this: Get the older kids ready to draw. Place the little one at the table with paper in front of him. Say, "I know you will draw *on the paper*. Markers and crayons are for drawing on *paper*." Supervise; the minute he starts to stray, remind him, "Where do we draw? On the paper." If he starts to rebel, firmly remove him from the art table, saying, "Markers are only for paper. I see you do not want to draw after all." Give him another chance the next day or later in the day. Ask, "If you want to use the markers, where will you use them?" Help him remember: On the *paper*. You can enlist your older kids to help reinforce this, if they're willing to without tattling. Whenever you catch him drawing on walls or wherever, firmly remove the pen and say, "Drawing is for *paper*. Now we will clean up the wall." Try to sound firm but not furious. This worked really well with our kids when they were two; we had a Play-Doh rule as well as a crayon and marker rule (if the Play-Doh fell on the floor more than three times, it was put away; it had to be used at the kitchen table, nowhere else).

A pacifier can be such a soothing thing to a baby—but don't make the mistake we did. We let our child become attached to an odd brand of pacifier. We were given two of them when our baby was born, and we never found out where they came from. Those two pacifiers are the only ones he's ever liked. We now live in fear of losing one or both.

⚬

I was trying to break my child of the pacifier habit. We all have a crutch, but jeez, I didn't want her to start high school dragging that thing with her. She was almost three. I tried one trick that I thought would work. I waited until she dropped it and then said, "Uh-oh, it's too dirty, we have to take it to be cleaned." She bought it! Then she pretty much forgot about it and just spent the night without it. Then, the next day, I said, "Ohhh, it's broken, we are going to have to get another one." She accepted this, I never produced a new one, and so far, she's forgotten all about it. That's the good thing about kids. They have a real short memory about things like that.

⚬

My toddler son used to scream and throw a temper tantrum every time I put him in his high chair, and I could never get him to eat. I thought he hated what I made for him, and I drove myself crazy trying to find something he liked. It wasn't until one day when I was over my mother's house, she didn't have a high chair, and he had to sit at the table with us bolstered by pillows that I realized that he just hated sitting in his chair. Maybe he had outgrown it. Now mealtimes are a lot more enjoyable because I've gotten a booster seat like you find at restaurants, and he loves sitting in it. We call it his special seat that no one else is allowed to use!

～⚙～

My daughter just turned eleven, and last year she had a brief course in fourth grade regarding puberty and menstruation. At that time, I bought a book for her called *What's Happening to My Body? Book for Girls* by Lynda Madaras. There's also one for boys. They cover everything! I gave it to her and told her I was also going to read it because I never had anything like it when I was her age! We've both read it on and off, and she's asked me questions, mostly about puberty and menstruation, but I expect there will be more questions about sex as she grows older. And although the book I gave her focuses on girls, there's also pretty much information about boys, so girls will have a good idea about what happens with them, too. I truly hope that this book and the discussions we've had so far will enable us to continue to talk about these important issues.

～⚙～

During puberty—be honest, answer questions. Don't make jokes about the body changes. Don't stare. Let them have privacy. Pack a cosmetic bag with the equipment a girl might need and let her keep that in the bottom of her backpack to have at school. Show her where the supplies are kept at home. Don't dwell on cramps and the pain periods are in general. Explain that every girl experiences periods, and it's no big deal. If you are proud of your body, your daughter will feel much more relaxed with the changes that she is experiencing in hers.

EATING

How do parents get kids to eat? Meal times can be arduous, especially when picky eaters are involved. In this section, moms spill their secrets on creative, appealing dishes for kids and problems with their own fussy eaters.

Do you want a tasty treat that your kids will love? Try this healthy and yummy snack: Between two pieces of toast, put [slices of] one peeled apple, cream cheese, applesauce, and a little cinnamon. My kids love it when I cut the sandwich into quarters, and they can pretend that they're having fancy hors d'oeuvres.

~◉~

A great summer treat that is fun and easy for kids to make is applesauce popsicles. I buy the Popsicle containers that you find in any department store, fill them with applesauce, and freeze them. You can use any kind of juice, too.

~◉~

My kids love to eat anything bite-sized. I found that cutting cheese or vegetables into cubes and sticking pretzel or potato sticks in them is a fun and healthy snack.

When I pick my child up from school at the end of the day, he is almost always hungry. That's why I always leave home with a little snack in the car. Not only does it satiate my son's hunger until mealtime, it makes for a pleasanter drive home for me.

My daughter takes her lunch to school in one of those insulated freezer bags. I found that the bag didn't stay cool enough for her lunch—I worried in particular about sandwiches with mayonnaise—so I found out a neat trick to keep her lunch cold. Now I always put a frozen drink in her bag. It keeps the rest of her lunch cold, and the beverage will be melted and ready to drink by lunchtime.

My daughter used to always bring juice boxes to school for her lunch until one day, I read the sugar content on the label. I couldn't believe it! I switched her to a milk carton, and now she and I are both happy!

My kids snack all the time, but I worry about junk food. I devised a fun between-meal treat that they really love.

I mix milk and food coloring that my kids "paint" on bread or bagels. Once I've toasted the foods, they come out rainbow-striped, making for fun and satisfying food that I can feel good about.

To avoid having formula go bad in the bottle without carrying around one of those heavy chill-packs (the type you keep in your freezer), use only powdered formula for bottles on the go. Just measure the correct amount of powder in the bottle, put on a nipple, cover with a cap, and all you need to do when your baby gets hungry is find a water fountain or a faucet to add water, stir, and serve.

This might go against the conventional wisdom, but I say avoid sippy cups in your move to get your child off the bottle and into drinking from glasses. I've seen so many children who are still using sippy cups at four and five and even six or seven. If you buy sturdy, well-balanced plastic cups and don't overfill them, and you help the child hold the cup steady at the beginning, they really will get the hang of drinking without spilling pretty quickly. If you baby them too long, they may figure they never have to be careful about spilling, and then you're stuck with those sippy tops for years.

My son won't drink milk. I knew he wasn't getting enough nutrition from fruit juices, so I tried chocolate milk, and he liked it. It's only a little bit sweeter than regular milk, and it has all the same nutrients, so we're both happy to have him drink it. I've also found apple juice and orange juice with added calcium and vitamins, and he drinks those—but only milk has protein, too.

I thought I would be able to breastfeed my daughter but found I couldn't. I was depressed about this for several months until I found a great book: *Bottlefeeding Without Guilt: A Reassuring Guide for Loving Parents* by Peggy Robin. Robin's book really saved my psyche. She explained how bottle-fed kids turn out just fine and that it's what the parents give in terms of love that really makes a difference for children. I highly recommend this book.

Weaning a baby from breast to bottle can be painful for the mom. Though the baby may adapt easily to sucking from an artificial nipple, the mom's breasts may not do so well without the baby keeping them emptied. The problem is called engorgement, and it can leave the breasts rock-hard and terribly sore. Prevention is the key. Plan to wean gradually over at least a four-week period. Eliminate one nursing every few days, starting with the midday one. Since you are more likely to wake up engorged after a night with no nursing, the last nursing to be eliminated should be the just-before-bedtime one. That is probably also the time your baby is most eager to keep nursing. If you do occasionally find yourself waking up feeling engorged, hand-express just enough milk to relieve the discomfort. More will only cause you to produce more milk. A long, warm shower or soak in the tub may also provide relief.

I thought I was going to give up breastfeeding because I couldn't handle it, but I stuck with it. I did end up getting so sore that I was bleeding at one point. Apparently, it is not that babies are hungry—they just need to suck. I was told "no pacifiers before six weeks" (nipple confusion), so I just ultimately stayed away from them, but I found that sometimes letting the baby suck on my little finger helped. Other times, nothing but nursing worked.

I'd like to help other breastfeeding moms who must travel for work avoid the mistake I made. In the few days before my first overnighter, I pumped out as many bottles of breast milk as I could for my baby. This left my baby well provided with bottles but made me get terribly engorged. All that pumping caused my breasts to step up production, and when I woke up the next morning, not having nursed or pumped the day or night before, my breasts were hard as a rock and painful. Next trip, I knew to start pumping just one extra bottle a day, several weeks ahead of time, and freeze the milk to be thawed by my sitter during my absence.

When eating at a restaurant: Be prepared! Bring a small snack, crayons, stickers, or something to keep the younger ones occupied. Ask the server to bring you the check and pay it as soon as the food arrives. That way, if your child has a meltdown, you're set. Sometimes we even ask for "to go" containers just in case. Finally, bring a wet washcloth in a Ziploc bag. It's perfect for really messy kids and even comes in handy for mom and dad.

Just a thought: This happened to a friend of mine and her three-year-old daughter. When she spoke to the nursery school nurses, they recommended putting fewer things into her lunchbox because too much choice can be intimidating. Now she puts in no more than three things, and the lunchbox comes home empty.

My son liked real food; he just had a rather refined gag reflex, so we gave him more practice. In other words, we offered him food whenever we could and prepared ourselves for it if he threw up. He learned eventually (it didn't take that long, about a month for it to wind down to occasionally) that he needed to chew his food and that he couldn't just swallow it right away as he did puréed food and milk.

⟶⬤◦

One mother shared a problem:
My four-year-old daughter just won't eat. She picks at her food and eventually feeds it to the dogs. She doesn't even eat the lunch I send with her to school. I am at my wits' end, trying everything to get her to eat. Should I just let her be or force her to eat?

Another mom responded:
You should probably double-check this with your doctor, but I'd say as long as she is gaining and maintaining the right weight for her age, don't worry. Give her a vitamin supplement just to cover your bases and let her nibble at her food. She may be going through a dormant growth stage, not needing as many calories, or she may just be too interested in other things to focus on food. Leave out lots of healthy snacks and let her nibble while she plays.

⟶⬤◦

Frozen grapes are still great healthy snacks. Take the stems off and pop them in the freezer. They taste just like little bits of grape Popsicle.

⟶⬤◦

One neat food trick I have found especially handy is what I call "portable dessert." I give the kids little ice cream cones full of candy and let them eat them on the way to errands that would otherwise not be fun. This way, they don't complain and are preoccupied when I have to, say, run to the grocery store.

My son is too young for school, but I pack him a little lunch anyway, and he's always thrilled. I put all kinds of little pictures and little colorful napkins in the bag and then he feels grown up like his sisters, who are a few years older. It also helps me out when I'm really busy because he can eat his lunch any time he wants.

Even with a toddler along, you can still enjoy a meal at a fairly nice restaurant. Just go early, no later than 6:30 P.M. The place will be fairly empty, and the waiters can seat you far away from other couples who might frown on a little one's noise. If there's no special children's menu, bring along dry cereal in a baggy, or ask for toast, a raw carrot, crackers, plain rice or plain spaghetti — something simple that the kitchen is likely to have on hand, and you know your toddler likes. Bring along your own toys, crayons, and paper. And be sure to ask for the check midway through your meal. You don't want to keep your small child cooped up in a high chair while you're waiting for coffee and dessert.

~⁂~

We take our five-year-old and our baby out to eat frequently but are careful about what kinds of places we take them to. We look for family-friendly places with lots of other babies and children, where the waiters know not to put filled glasses of water down in front of our infant or put a steaming hot plate within her reach. We favor places with outdoor seating and will often take turns walking around outside with her as we're waiting for our food. With lots of practice, our five-year-old has learned how to order on her own and has even been known to flag down our waiter to say, "We're ready for our check, please."

~⁂~

The only way my kids eat vegetables is when I'm able to sneak them in while they're unaware. Meat loaf is the best to get in a good amount. Tuna casserole also works, as does lasagna.

~⁂~

My toddler will frequently refuse the food I put on his plate, but I've learned the surest way to get him to try a new food is to put it on my own plate and when he reaches for it, say, "But that's Mommy's food! Are you sure you really want it?" The idea that it might be something special for grown-ups guarantees that he'll try it, and much of the time, after he has, he'll eat it. That's how I got him to like broccoli.

For a picky eater, it sometimes matters more how the food looks than how it tastes. I've found my picky eater is far more likely to try a new food if I present it in an interesting way or in an attractive dish. For example, my son would not touch cantaloupe until one day I served it cut up in a brandy glass. My daughter would never eat chunks of fresh pineapple, but when she was once served those canned pineapple rings, she loved them. Also, it seems to matter a lot if the foods are separate or part of another dish. My son will eat pizza with green pepper, onions, mushrooms, and almost anything else on it, but he would never eat a single one of those vegetables on its own, cooked or raw.

My children won't eat salads, but they will eat almost all the salad vegetables if they're served in the form of sticks for dipping. I put out a cup of French or ranch dressing in the center of a plate and arrange around it a circle of sticks of carrots, celery, green or red peppers, and sometimes even raw broccoli, and the kids love to dip them into the dressing and crunch on them as a course before dinner.

~✵~

My kids won't ordinarily eat carrots, but they will if I carve them into shapes. You can buy a little tool in a cookware store that turns carrots, cucumbers, and radishes into rosettes. You can also lay out asparagus sticks (steamed) in patterns to form a tick-tack-toe board and cut carrot circles to make *x*s and use sweet red onion circles as *o*s. Be sure your children know the rules: Playtime must be limited to a few minutes, and all game pieces have to be eaten in the end!

~✵~

I use cookie cutters to make fun shapes out of pieces of sliced American or cheddar cheese. My boys love to eat their cheese in the shape of dinosaurs, lions, gorillas, or other wild animals. They often prefer a snack of specially shaped cheese over cookies or other sweets.

~✵~

I like my children to eat a lot of yogurt because it has calcium and protein, and it's relatively low fat, but the type they like best is an expensive children's sort in very small containers that comes with a packet of candy sprinkles to mix in. Instead of buying this pricey kids' yogurt, I found I can buy the less expensive regular fruit yogurts

and buy a large container of sprinkles in the baking in-
gredients section of the supermarket, and the kids can
have sprinkles on their yogurts whenever they want at
half the price.

Holidays

Holidays can be very stressful times for parents and children. How can you keep the kids entertained with games and snacks during the Christmas season? What activities are fun for a birthday? How can the situation be more relaxing for mom and dad? This section addresses ways to make the holidays easier on kids and parents and provides ideas for fun crafts and treats for the whole family.

For small children's birthday parties, think small! I know it's tempting to invite every little friend your child ever met, but it really will be much more fun for all if you keep it to a manageable number. That way, there will be no long waits for turns at pin-the-tail-on-the-donkey or other games. For two- and three-year-olds, six children is about the maximum. Four-year-olds might have seven or eight guests, and five-year-olds, ten or twelve. At six and older, you can safely invite the whole class.

The holiday season can be really crazy for preschoolers and younger children. To keep them from being overwhelmed, we've changed the Christmas tradition a bit. We tell them that Santa brings their stockings, and we're sure to fill them with all sorts of fun things so they'll be a surprise on Christmas morning. The week leading up to Christmas, we open a few packages a day. That way, they can thank the person who gave them, play with them, and appreciate each gift. Otherwise, they open the first gift on Christmas morning and can't get past it to the others.

When you have crawling or toddling children in the house, you either need to put your Christmas tree inside a playpen or hang only baby-safe ornaments on the lower branches. It's probably a good idea to measure your child's longest reach and add two or three inches to arrive at a safe height for hanging your delicate glass ornaments.

My tip is entitled "The Christmas List."

The Christmas List

Holidays fill the air with excitement. When my children were young, I knew they were just beginning to build their own personal memory banks of Christmas experiences. I was aware that "what we do today will be remembered for many tomorrows." As a mother, I wanted to avoid disappointment on Christmas morning when the much-anticipated package would be opened, only to be received with disappointment. The toy may not turn out to be what my children had imagined from the wonders of television. This is how I solved the problem.

When my children were old enough to begin to ask for what they saw on television, I had them make their "want" lists. But with that, our journey into making the Christmas list was just beginning. One Saturday morning after breakfast, we climbed into the car with our lists and headed for the store. Patiently, we went up and down the aisles searching for each item. One by one, we would look at the toys, examining them carefully to see if they really were as good as what we had seen on television. We discussed the toy, the color, the size, and the price. Surprisingly, before they could fully comprehend the value of money, they were able to make value judgments about whether one toy was worth more than another. We made lots of notes on the list. Sometimes we even added toys that we had not seen on television.

I could hear the disappointment in their voices

when they said, "Mommy, this isn't like what I saw on television." But I could also hear the excitement when they found a toy that really did what the commercial promised, and they could hardly wait to play with it.

After returning home they rewrote their "want" lists. They thought about what they had seen and learned before prioritizing their final lists. Some items were scratched off completely. But now they knew exactly what they were asking for.

I learned it is far less traumatic to reveal a false illusion of a toy that is perched on a shelf in a toy store than to see the face of disappointment on a child sitting under a tree on Christmas morning.

Holiday meals are a lot easier on everyone if you can time them to coincide with the baby's nap. Let relatives and friends who want to see the baby do all their lap holding and playing early on, while the baby is still active and not yet overstimulated and cranky. Then firmly announce that it's the baby's nap time and remove her from the sight and sound of all the goings-on. If you're visiting a relative's house, put the baby down in a Portacrib she's used before and is familiar with. A special blanket or stuffed animal may help her fall asleep in an unfamiliar room. If the celebration is at your house, try to follow your usual routine about napping as closely as possible. Don't let other relatives "help" you put the baby down — that will only give her the idea that there are lots of new people still in the house, and she could be missing out on something if she naps.

~◉◉~

In some of our past big families get-togethers at Christmas or other gift-giving holidays, we've found that we ended up with an unmanageable mountain of toys, which left the small kids overwhelmed and the bigger kids greedy and ungrateful. Here's what's worked for us to tame the over giving problem: Some weeks prior to the holiday, we have a drawing from a hat. Each adult who will be celebrating Christmas at our house must draw a child's name from the hat. That adult buys a present for that child only. Adults do not buy presents for each other. Children who are old enough to make presents may make them and wrap them for their own parents only. No presents will be exchanged between children. This way, the emphasis is on being with family and giving something special that you have had time to think about — not on how much loot you're going to get.

MEDICAL TIPS

Is there anything more frightening than a sick child? Or worse, a child with a condition parents can't identify? Much as we try to avoid it, at one time or another, parents will be confronted by a child's medical problem. This section not only focuses on serious problems but also has tips on everyday maladies.

Don't let your baby get into the habit of falling asleep with a bottle in his mouth. Our dentist told us that milk remaining on the teeth at night can cause cavities and even loss of the primary teeth, a condition known as "baby-bottle mouth" or "nursing caries." Our baby had become used to a last bottle before bedtime, but now that we're aware of the pitfalls, we fill his last bottle with plain water.

～❀～

If you're trying to get your baby to take liquid Tylenol mixed with fruit juice in a bottle, use an opaque bottle. That way, your baby can't tell by the color of the liquid that anything's changed. The slight change in flavoring is much more likely to be accepted if the baby believes that she's getting something she's had and liked before.

⁓

Those ear thermometers are wonderful once you learn the technique of using them properly. You get a fairly accurate reading in only two seconds, and children are generally used to the idea of a medical instrument that goes in the ear. You and your spouse should practice on each other when your own temperatures are normal until you can consistently get the correct reading.

⁓

There's a wonderful new type of baby thermometer on the market that's contained in a pacifier. The baby sucks on the pacifier for a minute, and colored dots on the end change to green or brown, registering the baby's temperature. Although it's not as accurate as a rectal reading, it sure is a lot easier, and it works well enough to let you know if your baby is about normal, has a moderate fever, or a high one.

⁓

If your child has been prescribed an antibiotic in liquid form, see if your pharmacist can mix in a special flavor that you know your child likes. Cherry or bubblegum flavorings are popular, but if your child doesn't like either of those two, ask your pharmacist about others. A few pharmacists specialize in mixing up medicines for children, and if you've found it difficult to get your child to take medicine, it might be worthwhile calling around in your city to find out if any pharmacy offers a wide variety of flavorings. We found a pharmacy that let our toddler "taste-test" the mixing bases and pick the flavor she liked best. The pharmacist also gave us tips about what flavors best disguised the taste of the antibiotic our child had to take.

Many kids are terrified at the prospect of having a Band-Aid removed. Try rubbing a little mineral oil around the sides and top of the Band-Aid, and it should slide right off without pulling.

If you know your baby or toddler is going to be getting a shot at the doctor's, try giving a dose of infant Tylenol just *before* you go. Although it won't make the injection any less painful, it will reduce any reaction he might otherwise have to the shot (such as fever, swelling at the injection site, or later pain). Of course, you should discuss this with your doctor before you try it.

Head lice are one of the most difficult problems I've ever had to face as a mother of a kindergartner — and one I never expected to encounter. I quickly learned that those over-the-counter remedies are not terribly effective. The best thing to do was just to keep combing the child's head several times a day with a special fine-toothed lice comb. You can get rid of most of the eggs that way, but the only sure way to kill them all is very messy: Take Vaseline or some other brand of petroleum jelly and coat the child's scalp in the evening just before bedtime. Cover the child's hair with a plastic shower cap, and the lice will all be killed by morning. The only trouble with this method is that it may take daily shampoos for several days running to completely get all the gooey mess out of your child's hair.

One mom needed a solution for a scalp condition:
My six-week-old daughter has a lot of flaky, cream-colored gunk on her head. I try to brush it off, and I do get some, but most of it stays! It looks like dandruff, but I believe it's cradle cap.

Another mom responded:
Both of my boys had cradle cap in the few weeks after birth. I got rid of it by gently rubbing their heads with an old toothbrush while using baby shampoo to carry the flakes away. It took a few days of this light scrubbing, but it went away. I've also been told to rub a bit of baby oil in the scalp and shampoo as usual.

-◈-

One mother had a son who suffered from very bad colic. The doctor did not believe in using medicine to treat it.

Another mom came to the rescue with some good advice:
I discovered that my son had dietary sensitivities to dairy products, soy, and egg, which I could not eat at all until he was seventeen-months-old. We tested this every month or so, and every time I had any, he would be up for three nights screaming. (It takes a week for dairy to get out of your system and for you to see a difference.) We also tried massage, but the diet was the only thing to work. It was a good thing that we were breastfeeding, as formulas are made up of dairy and soy. Max was also very difficult at night, I think because of the gas problems (when he was lying down, the gas couldn't get up) and would sleep only if right next to me, which enabled us all to sleep a bit. We had never even considered the "family bed" thing, but it really made life easier for all of us.

-◈-

When your child is sick and has been experiencing nausea, you know you will very likely be up several times during the night, changing the sheets. Though you may not be able to alleviate her queasy tummy, you can at least make the bed-cleaning process quick and simple and less stressful for both parent and child. Here's how: Take a large beach towel and place it smoothly over the bottom sheet on the top half of the bed. Tuck in at the sides. Your child should lie on it and then you cover her with the top sheet and blanket, as usual. Over the blanket lay another very large beach towel. Tuck both the blanket and beach towel in at the same time. Keep in easy reach a few clean nightgowns, pillowcases, and beach towels so that when your child throws up in bed, you just take away everything that's soiled, without having to remake the bed. Also be sure to keep a large wastebasket lined with a plastic bag right beside the bed.

My little boy used to get an ear infection with every cold or flu until I learned about elevating his head at night. Fluid from his stuffy nose tends to flow back to his ears when he's sleeping, but if the head of his bed is slightly raised, this is prevented, and he's far less likely to get an infection. Before he turned two, we did not let him sleep with a pillow but raised the head of his crib by slipping thick carpet-protector squares under the two front legs of his crib.

My daughter was always terrified of the doctor's office — though she seemed to like the doctor pretty well. At last I figured out that it was the examining table that scared her most of all. It was too high, and she hated being put down on that scratchy paper covering. Now she sits in my lap for most of the exam. When she has to lie down, I put down a soft baby blanket from home on top of the examining table paper, and she's much better about lying down on it.

⟶◉⟵

Before our child's first visit to the dentist, my husband and I put on a little skit and acted out all the things the dentist and the hygienist would do at her check-up. We made sure she understood that there are no shots at a dental check-up and that all she'd have to do was open her mouth and show off her teeth when asked. She loved our little play, and I think it really helped because when we arrived, she climbed right up into the examining chair and opened her mouth wide. It helped, of course, that after the visit the dentist let her pick out a little prize from a box. She can't wait to go back for her next check-up.

⟶◉⟵

If your child has had more than two or three ear infections, it might be worth your while to purchase a home otoscope. While your child is healthy, practice viewing inside his or her ears to see what they look like when normal. Whenever your child develops symptoms of an infection, such as ear pain, feeling of stuffiness, or fever, take your child to the doctor as usual. If the doctor confirms the diagnosis of an ear infection, you can use your otoscope to look in your child's ear daily and check to see if the prescribed treatment appears to be taking care of the problem.

~♦~

Forget those high-priced diaper rash ointments. Petroleum jelly works better than all of them. Just make sure the baby's bottom is completely dry before you put it on.

~♦~

I've found the easiest way to get my toddler to take Tylenol is to buy the grape-flavored drops and add them to a small bottle of grape juice.

~♦~

No matter what I did, I couldn't get my daughter to take her medicine off a spoon — even if it was flavored like bubblegum or grape juice. Finally, I asked my doctor about combining it with food. My daughter loves applesauce. My doctor prescribed the medicine in capsule form, then showed me how to break open the capsules and mix the medicine in with the applesauce. We make sure she can't see the medicine granules in each spoonful. We also make sure the medicine is swallowed in the first three or four bites, to be sure she has gotten the full dose, even if she doesn't eat all of the applesauce. Of course, you should always check with your doctor to make sure this trick will work with the medicine your child has been prescribed.

It's so much easier to give medicine when the child knows how to swallow a pill. I wanted to see if my four-year-old could do it, so I bought a bag of M&M's and asked him to try to swallow one without chewing it. He had no problem with it. The next time his doctor prescribed a medication, I asked the doctor if it came in pill form and if the pill was smaller than an M&M. Since then, my son hasn't had to struggle with liquid medicines.

NEW SCHOOL

Starting a new school can be very traumatic for children. Here, mothers share secrets on making the first day a little easier.

To get a small child to look forward to the start of preschool or daycare, find out whether there will be some activity that the child hasn't been able to do at home. I was told that my child's nursery school had a big easel and paints, so I deliberately didn't keep paints in our house. That way, on the very first day, I walked her over to the easel and said, "Would you like to paint?" and since it was a new and exciting activity to her, she went to it right away. She got so into her painting that she barely noticed when I said goodbye. I saw many children ignoring the school's art supplies and play equipment. They had all these things at home already, and in some cases, even bigger and better things, so there was nothing to entice them about their new school—so all they had to focus on was the fact that their parents were leaving.

If your child is going to be starting at a new school, call the principal to find out if you and your child can get a tour of the building and the classroom a few days before the first day. Being familiar with the building will go a long way to easing any first-day jitters.

Always let your child pick out as many of his own school supplies as possible. It's comforting to bring along a favorite lunchbox or backpack when a child first goes off to a strange new place. Also, if possible let your child wear his favorite outfit on the first day.

If your child is going into a new school and won't know the other children, see if you can get a list of names and telephone numbers of classmates a few weeks ahead of time. Arrange a play date, perhaps two or three, with some other children from the class so that when the first day comes your child will know someone.

PRIVATE TIME

Everyone needs a little time to themselves. Moms, dads, and even kids need a special time and place to get away from the pressures and frustrations of everyday life. Whether to recover from screaming siblings or a jam-packed, stressful day, all members of the family need their private time.

My husband coaches our son's Little League baseball games, and this often makes our daughter feel left out. So we have a special day together when we do girly things that neither my husband nor my son wants to do—shopping or playing with dolls or dressing up. This doesn't make my son feel left out because he doesn't want to be doing those things anyway, and it makes my daughter feel like she, too, is special.

⚜

A suggestion for getting some privacy for parents. Take the "penny jar" and pour the entire contents in a sandbox. Tell the child how much money they should find (so maybe you're wrong) and not to stop until they have found it all.

⁓⁓⁓

I am a big fan of the "special place." My younger son used to go after my older son's toys all the time and follow him around constantly. It was causing all kinds of fights and tantrums. So I set up a corner of the living room with blankets, toys, and stuff just for my older son. It is a place for him to go that is just for him.

⁓⁓⁓

At least once a month, I make sure to do something special alone with each of my three children. The child gets to pick the activity for his or her "date" with Mom. That way we get to know each other as individuals, not just as parents and children. The kids really look forward to their time alone with me and use it to let me in on what's really most important to each one of them.

⁓⁓⁓

Though my husband works regular hours, and I stay home with our baby, he makes sure I always can get a little time to myself each day, if only to be able to take a shower in peace or read in bed. He usually takes the baby out for an early morning and late evening stroll. He enjoys his time alone with the baby, and I am always glad that I can count on some relaxing moments on my own.

QUICK CLEANUP

The words "quick cleanup" can seem like a contradiction to many mothers and fathers. Since much of a parent's day is spent cleaning up after toddlers' spills and "art work" on the walls, any extra information on time-saving solutions is much appreciated. With the following advice, parents share their harrowing tales of messy disasters and tricks for a cleaner and neater house.

It used to be a nightmare to clean up my child after a meal. Warm washcloths were the best, but I didn't want to wait for the water to warm up. Sometimes a few seconds make all the difference when you have to do the same thing every meal. So I figured out a way to speed this up. Soak a washcloth and pop it in the microwave for a few seconds, and you have an instant hot cloth.

In order to get my child to wash his hands, I have taken to having him count to a certain number or recite the alphabet. That way I know he's been at the sink long enough. Otherwise, his hands would barely touch the water. We have even tried singing little refrains from songs as a timer.

⟿

Have you ever noticed it is almost impossible to get marks and food off your kids? How do they get that stuff on themselves so permanently? If you rub Vaseline on their faces before they eat, it is so much easier to wipe off the food. Also, peanut butter really gets marks off the skin.

⟿

I learned a nifty tip when I was in the hospital recently. I didn't know how to wash my baby's hair. She seemed so delicate and tiny. One nurse showed me how to do it right. Get a squirt bottle and fill it with water. After soaping up the little one's head, squirt instead of rinsing. Not only is it gentler, with just enough pressure, but they love the squirting. They think it is a game.

⟿

Here's an easy cleanup tip. It may sound strange, but after you use it, you'll thank me! Put a coffee filter in the potty cup during training, and when they're done each time, throw the filter in the trash. Minimal mess!

⟿

I have a great tip for flyaway hair. In the wintertime, there can be alot of static build-up, and I could never figure out a good way to avoid it. Finally, I heard that if you spritz a mix of conditioner and water onto your child's hair, it will keep the frizzies away. It also works to spray Static Guard on a hairbrush, which makes your hair very shiny, too.

⚬

If you live in a house with more than one level, establish a baby-changing station on each level. You'll really save yourself endless running up and down stairs if you keep a changing pad and diaper supplies in a few different parts of the house.

⚬

Those plastic bags from the grocery store have 1,001 uses: line small trash pails; carry a few in the car for dirty diapers, muddy shoes, or car trash; pack lunch, separate stuff for errands (library books in one, clothes for the cleaner in another).

⚬

Don't spend a lot of money on fancy bibs! They all start to look yucky after a few weeks of use. The easiest, most practical solution I found was to buy large dish towels, drape them around the baby, and clip them in the back with a large binder clip, hair clip, or clothespin.

⚬

The Chubs baby wipe containers are really useful once they're empty. The containers are stackable and come in bright, primary colors, so they make good-looking, convenient bins for many things: small toys, puzzle parts, hair accessories, bath supplies, bath toys, art supplies—you name it. I used to save shoe boxes for all these things, but Chubs boxes snap tight and don't spill out when a toddler dumps them over!

Babies in high chairs sometimes hate having their faces wiped off after eating—yet they almost always need it. Here are two possible solutions: Hand the baby a damp washcloth, and in the course of playing with it, she'll almost certainly bring it to her mouth and end up wiping herself clean; or take her out of the high chair, bring her over to the kitchen sink, and splash some warm water on her face and hands yourself (then the cleaning up will seem like playtime to her).

When your baby boy is on the diaper table, right after you take the diaper off, drape a washcloth over his penis, so you won't get squirted if he starts to pee again. This is especially a good precaution to take with newborns, who are unpredictable, and can really spray you when you least expect it.

I collect all the perfumed advertising pages I find inside fashion magazines. I don't use them on myself but drop them into the diaper pail as deodorizers.

Very young children can help with the laundry. I've found the best job for them is pulling out all the socks. When they're toddlers, they can just find all socks and heap them in a pile. When they're a little older, they can match pairs and even roll them together.

Here's a quick and easy trick to help cope with a baby who kicks while you're changing his diaper. Gently grab hold of his ankles and make his legs pedal in a circle as if he's bicycling. He'll probably like this motion and start laughing and stop kicking. If he doesn't like it, he'll put his legs down. Either way, he'll stop kicking.

Those plastic carryalls that you can buy to hold cleaning supplies make excellent portable toy baskets. When off on a visit to an adult who may not have a lot of things to keep your child amused, fill up the carryall with favorite playthings, markers, coloring books, and so forth, and let your child pick and choose activities to amuse herself, leaving the adults in peace.

For stains, the local consignment shop recommends using a mixture of one-half color-safe bleach and one-half stain remover. They have also come out with a new stain remover made especially for white clothes that has bleach in it. You can also use shampoo on protein stains.

Never buy children's clothes that say "hand-wash only." If someone gives you a present that isn't machine-washable, either give it away, or machine-wash it and take your chances. Half the time the hand-washables hold up just fine in the washer and dryer, and you've saved yourself hours of aggravation sorting and hand-washing clothes that your kids are going to wear out or grow out of in a few months anyway.

For kiddie birthdays, skip the big cake. Make cupcakes for the two-and-under set. Lay out a big blanket (outside if the weather permits) and put the kids on the blanket. They'll devour their cupcakes, and when they're done, you just have to shake out the blanket, fold it up, and toss it in the laundry. If you're really clever you'll have a kiddie pool ready to go, and all the kids can go for a dip afterwards to get cleaned up. Voila! A mess-free party!

Baby wipes have multiple uses—they are great for baby stains on clothes. What do you do if baby spits up or throws up on your clothes? Just use a baby wipe on that silk, wool, or whatever, and it's all gone.

I have an amazing discovery I want to share with all moms! Mix one cup Clorox II powder and one cup of Cascade powdered dishwasher detergent together in a bucket and add the hottest water you can. Throw the clothes in the bucket and soak all night. Presto! The stains are gone! It really is magic!

For quick clean-ups, buy a big package of plain white washcloths. Keep them handy at all times for quick cleaning after meals, playtime, or even spills. You use them once and toss them in the laundry. That way, you always have a fairly sterile cloth and don't have to waste paper towels (which never do the job properly anyway, let's face it!).

To wash stuffed animals, dolls, and other delicates with cloth or plastic parts, put them in a pillowcase (tied shut), wash in cold water and rinse, use the gentle cycle, if you have one, to dry them, and let it lie out in the sun for the day. I have also heard that specialty doll stores have a special cleaner for the vinyl faces.

Like most little ones, my daughter has hundreds of stuffed animals! We didn't want to just shove them in a closet, but we didn't want to leave them lying around and getting in the way, either. We didn't know what to do! Then my husband had a stroke of genius. He bought a long piece of chain and attached it to the ceiling, then hung the animals from it all the way to the ground. Every so often we try something else, like hanging each stuffed animal from a separate piece of string or chain all over the ceiling. It looks like it's raining teddy bears!

~⚬~

My kids have so many stuffed animals we had to put in new shelves just for them. They are high enough so that they look decorative, but they are also fun for the kids because they can finally view all the stuffed animals they have at once.

~⚬~

The only way to get my daughter to keep her room clean is to threaten her toys with jail time. If there are any toys left on the bedroom floor at the end of the day, the toy spends the night in jail. The only way to spring Bugs is to do chores around the house.

~⚬~

Toy boxes are a fun way to keep toys out of the way so the children's rooms aren't always disaster areas. If you keep several boxes around, you can switch the toys that are played with from time to time. This way, they seem new again.

~⚬~

Be careful of those small accessories that come with fashion dolls and other toys. Young children could choke on them. One way to avoid this is to keep all the pieces in a toolbox or any container with a compartmentalized lid. These sections can safely hold the smaller items. Have fun with the box itself. Color it or cover it with stickers. Your child may remember to use it more.

We used to have one of those plastic floor-protector mats under the high chair, but it was harder to clean all the spills off it than to clean the floor. Someone suggested we buy a small plastic wading pool and put that under the high chair. That's worked wonderfully to catch all the mess. It generally wipes clean, but if there's a really big spill in it, I just put it out in the backyard and hose it off.

I've found dozens of uses for my husband's old unwanted t-shirts. I often throw one on over my own clothes to have an instant protective smock. Or I just toss one over my shoulder as a protective burping cloth. Old t-shirts make excellent painting smocks for preschoolers and grade-schoolers. Even after the sleeves are full of holes, you can cut out the front and keep the neck to make a great baby's bib.

Instead of hauling around a big diaper bag full of supplies, I use what I call diaper kits that are small enough to be stuffed inside a good-sized pocketbook. A diaper kit consists of a gallon-sized plastic zipper bag containing the following: one or two disposable diapers, a little packet of travel wipes, a travel-sized packet of tissues, and a few individually sealed packages of Wash'n Dries or Wet-Naps to clean your hands afterwards, just in case there isn't a sink with soap nearby. For a changing pad, bring along about ten undivided sheets of paper toweling, folding them to the size you need for your baby. If you don't want to use and then throw out so much paper toweling each time, you could instead buy a plastic-coated, flannel-backed picnic tablecloth and cut it into changing-pad-sized lengths. After each use, the pad could be cleaned with a baby-wipe and refolded into your purse.

My child's nursery school taught me a valuable lesson about extra clothing. Just as it makes sense to keep a complete set of extra clothes at the child's school in case of accidents, it's worthwhile keeping a complete set in the trunk of your car at all times. I've also given my parents a few extra pairs of underpants and an extra set of leggings, so that if any accidents happen at Grandma and Grandpa's house, it's no big deal.

I could never figure out how to keep my kids from mixing up all the puzzle pieces. Now I separate the puzzles and put each into its own plastic bag. Once my children are done with one puzzle, they have to put it away before they can take out another. You can never have too much organization.

❧

You can use those net bags that are usually used for hosiery for washing toys in the dishwasher. If you have dolls or anything with little plastic parts, put them in the bag. This way they won't fly all over the dishwasher. Be careful and keep the bag on the top shelf because the hot coil is on the bottom, and you don't want to melt anything.

❧

One way to keep little ones from being bored with old toys is to exchange. Trade with other families in your neighborhood. This probably will keep kids from getting upset over how Jimmy's toys are better, because now they are almost communal! Don't forget to put your initials on the toys so you will remember whose is whose.

❧

Here are some useful ways to remove stains, a problem all mothers face: Soak clothes in the sink overnight with a little stain remover; mix baking soda and water as an easy stain lifter for furniture; use club soda on urine stains on carpets.

I heard this tip from a mother I knew from my son's playgroup: Put white rice and water in your baby's empty bottle and shake it thoroughly. This lifts that nasty milk ring.

RECREATION

It's Friday, and parents everywhere are thinking, "What is the family going to do this weekend? How can we entertain the kids for two whole days?" Or, if you are a parent who has had a recent weekend trauma, you might be thinking, "How do I avoid making the same mistake this time?" Families need to be together enjoying stimulating activities and having quality time, especially activities that are fun for the whole family. In this section, parents share ideas for family fun, plus the ups and downs of vacations past.

When vacationing with children, remember this: Write a list for everything. It sounds silly, but it is crucial. Write a specific list of activities and trips to take with your family that includes everybody's quirks. Is Molly afraid of water? Is Jack bad on planes? These are things to remember. On your list, keep track of everything that would be required for the trip; every tent, Band-Aid, and flashlight should be accounted for. This helps put things into perspective. During each vacation, keep a list of good activities to do and a list of bad ones. This way, when summer rolls around again, and you think to yourself how much fun it would be to hike through the mountains, the list will remind you of how difficult that trip was for the whole family. And you can always refer to the good-trip list and repeat a winner!

—⚬—

I worry a lot about my family and I being eaten alive when camping. I was always the one bugs went after! Most of the time I sprayed the clothes with bug spray and then dressed the kids, but this time I tried something new. I sprayed handkerchief-sized pieces of cloth and then tied them around their necks. It worked great, and they looked like little cowboys and cowgirls. Handkerchiefs are the best for other stuff, too. I bring them with me everywhere. They are good for runny noses, little accidents, food on the face, and lots of things.

—⚬—

The strangest thing happened on my family's first camping trip. We had been out on the water canoeing for about fifteen minutes, and my young daughter announced she no longer wanted to be there. She then threw her legs over the edge and jumped into the water! Luckily, my husband grabbed her by the life jacket and hauled her into the canoe in a matter of seconds. She was fine, no worries there, but she looked more surprised than anything else. It never in my wildest dreams occurred to me that could happen. I was not prepared for it. At least we know she isn't afraid of the water!

My husband and I highly recommend tandem-bike recreation. When you have little ones, it's great because you can attach a trailer, and that way both parents are helping tow them. When they get too big for that, we are going to get a "stoker kit." It essentially extends the pedals so the child can reach them. The tandem keeps us together and also eliminates the problem of having the kids riding solo in heavy traffic, going down big hills, and that stuff.

When going on canoe trips, it is crucial to bring life jackets for everyone. It is very likely that everyone (kiddies) will hate them, but they are essential. The hard part with kids is that the jackets are so heavy. The best way to deal with this is to get lots of practice trying them on before getting in the water. Make sure to reinforce what a good job they are doing so they don't get cranky and fussy.

It's fun to take your child to the skating rink for the first time, but to make it easier on everyone, I advise making sure you have a ratio of two adults (who know how to skate) for each child—one adult to hold each of the child's hands. You function like a pair of training wheels.

As the child finds his balance, first one adult lets go on one side. Then as he's gaining confidence, the other lets go of his other hand, and away he goes—skating.

When teaching your child to ride a bicycle, don't steady the bike by holding on to the back of the seat. Have the child wear a zipped-up jacket. Get a good grip on the back of the jacket and run behind the bike, using your grip on the jacket to apply just enough stabilizing force to help the child balance. Loosen your grip as you feel your child stabilize, and back away altogether when you find yourself no longer applying any corrective balance. Your child will be biking solo in no time.

The first time we left our son with his grandparents for several nights, we also left them with a handmade booklet called *The Book of Jeffrey* with all the details they needed for taking care of him. It was made of loose-leaf pages in a small binder so that as Jeffrey grew, and the information changed, we could pull out a page with outdated information and substitute another. My parents loved having this quick reference guide on hand in case of trouble, and we felt reassured to know that we had covered almost any question they might have had about his care while we were away. Even Jeffrey seemed reassured to know that his grandparents could look in *The Book of*

Jeffrey to find out how Mommy and Daddy always did something and do it just the same way in our absence.

~◦~

We think it's important to see a babysitter in action before leaving our child with her all day while we are at work. If we like someone we've interviewed, we invite her to come and babysit on a Saturday or Sunday when we are home. That way, we can get a pretty good sense of how she interacts with our child. We don't hover around. After we've shown her around the house, we go off and do yard work or other activities, but drop in on her and our child every so often to see how they're getting along. With a trial day, we can see how the babysitter deals with problems, like getting our child to eat lunch (she's a very picky eater) and take a nap. It's happened more than once that we've been very impressed with someone after an interview but far from confident in her abilities after seeing her at work for a few hours. Of course we always pay for the time worked, whether or not we ultimately hire the sitter for the full-time job.

~◦~

Pop-up and pull-the-flap books are wonderful, but they don't last very long when you've got an active toddler in the house. Instead of keeping them out of reach, reinforce the movable parts with tape, and they should stand up through some pretty rough wear-and-tear. Of course, whenever you read a pop-up book to your little one, you should also show them how to pull the tabs gently so that they can enjoy the book for a long time to come.

~⊛~

Put on some background music when you videotape your babies or children playing together. Music tends to spice up the activity, and it will make the tapes more interesting to watch later.

~⊛~

Stop taking pictures if the baby seems to be getting cranky or uncooperative. You'll just waste film. Better to wait patiently for another occasion. If you keep your camera loaded and easily available, you'll be able to snatch it up and shoot when the time is right.

~⊛~

The best way to prevent red-eye in your children's photographs is to avoid using the flash whenever possible. Even the anti-red-eye features on cameras only work some of the time. You're better off taking mostly outdoor pictures or shooting indoors without the flash, using high-speed film, after you've adjusted the light for maximum brightness. If your shots still come out too dark, you can ask the photo lab to lighten up any that you want to reprint.

~⊛~

Catalogs, especially for baby clothes and toys, are very diverting for toddlers to look through. Whenever I pick up the mail, the first thing I do is hand any interesting catalogs to my son and tell him that's his mail. While he's sitting and flipping through the pages, I have a chance to read my mail and sometimes even pay my bills.

There is always a way to make learning fun. If your kids aren't interested in reading, make it a big event to go to the library. Luckily, my children really loved to read and listen to stories being read to them, but they really got into it when we started going to the library. Make it their special day. Show them how much fun it is to have a library card and go to the events put on by the library, like kids' story hour. It will feel like a grown-up, fun thing to do. Bookstores host similar events like story hours and song hours, and they're a lot of fun for adults, too.

Libraries are now offering many more services than in the past, and most are free. You can even borrow videos, CDs, and tapes.

ABC Fun Project: I use old magnetic-style photo albums for a fun ABC project. On every third page I put a large letter—A, B, C, and so on. When I'm finished reading my magazines or before I throw out color brochures, I look for pictures of things that begin with those letters. If I find a great tiger, I cut it out and add it to the "*t*" page. I label the tiger and go back for more pictures. Right now my girls can just point to the object and identify it. Down the road, they'll be practicing their reading skills. The best part is that it's all made out of recycled stuff!

A fun thing to start with a new baby is take a picture of him on the same chair every month next to a blackboard that says, "I'm three months old today, May 1997." When they're a year old, you'll have a chronicle of how they've grown, and it's neat to have them framed for others to admire.

People with young children should never again have to spend money on birthday cards. Just keep a supply of colored construction paper on hand and assign your kids the job of card making. Even the youngest toddlers can decorate a card. Just give them some of those baby-safe rolling paints (they look like roll-on deodorants, but they dispense the colors neatly), hand them a sheet of the folded construction paper, and watch them work. For a card from the whole family, dip each member's palm in paint and leave a hand print.

To make sure your child knows her phone number, make up a simple rhyme that's easy to recite and remember. For example:

555-9133

That is how you can call me!

Don't throw out all your junk mail. To your kids it isn't junk at all—it's a source of fun and information. Catalogs have colored pictures the kids can cut out and use to make collages and cards; wildlife organizations often include animal stickers and pitch-letters with facts about endangered species; window envelopes can be cut and turned into a pair of goggles or the clear plastic can be removed and cut to make flower petals or colored to make "stained-glass" windows.

When the weather's awful, and the kids can't go outside and play, try letting them have a camp-out indoors. Make a tent by draping a bed sheet over two kitchen chairs. If you have a fireplace, make a fire and let them roast marshmallows over the "campfire" (under your close supervision, of course).

You don't need to buy your toddler one of those stacking sets designed by "child development experts." Just use your graduated set of storage containers. Your child will have just as much fun nesting the containers inside each other or stacking them up on top of each other as he would with the expensive play stackers—and when he's done with them, you can wash them off and use them to store food.

※

Here's a game our eighteen-month-old used to enjoy more than anything: It's called "box-sledding." You need a large-sized cardboard shipping box that's big enough to seat your toddler comfortably. Make sure you remove any staples or packing Styrofoam. Attach a long piece of twine to each of the corners of one of the short sides of the box to form a pulling loop, as on a sled. Sit your toddler in the box on a carpeted floor in a long hall or large room. Pull your toddler around the room. She will yell "Wheee!" and cry, "More, more!" whenever you're ready to stop. It's guaranteed fun for hours (though you will probably tire of being the sled dog long before your toddler tires of getting a ride).

※

When my children were around three years old, I'd ask them every so often to tell me a story. I'd sit at the computer keyboard and type exactly what the child said, word for word, without any editing. Some of these stories were so charming and funny, I'd copy them for relatives or read them aloud to the grandparents over the telephone. Years later, when the child wants to know what he was like during his toddler years, I have the stories to show him. They're a wonderful keepsake for relatives, too.

I used to save empty tissue boxes, the kind that had an oval slot at the top to pull out the tissues, to create a wonderful homemade discovery game to play with my toddler. I would put an object in the box without letting her see it, and she had to guess what it was, first by the sound of it shaking in the box and second after putting her hand through the slot and feeling it without looking. Good objects were blocks, dandelions or other soft flowers, dry foods, smooth stones, or crumpled-up balls of paper. This game teaches them about shapes, sizes, and sounds, as well as encouraging them to make guesses and know the names of things.

Babies who can sit up love this game, which I call "Bowling for Babies." Sit your baby on a carpet or other soft, flat surface with her legs out in front of her, feet wide apart. Gently roll a tennis ball or a medium-sized plastic or rubber ball to her from a short distance away. You can aim the ball straight at her or try to bank it against one of her legs. She'll quickly learn to catch it and roll it back to you. This game can keep her amused for a long time, especially if you devise variations, such as using two balls, rolling the ball into a box, or trying to knock a toy over with the ball.

Want a simple way to impress your kids? Learn three or four easy magic tricks. You don't have to be particularly dexterous — just go to any novelty store and buy a magic set that includes some easy-to-manipulate props. Make a coin disappear and reappear or correctly pick out the card they have chosen from a deck, and you will seem incredibly powerful in their eyes — at least while they're very young.

Here's a rainy-day amusement anyone can do: Draw faces on your hands. Remember Señor Wences, who used to do an act on *The Ed Sullivan Show*? He drew eyes on either side of the first knuckle of his forefinger and made lips with lipstick on the edges where his thumb moved against the side of his hand. Demonstrate on your own hand and then make funny faces on your kids' hands. A child home sick can make the "mouths" on either hand talk to each other for hours.

My son often wants to be involved with the grown-up toys in the house, but sometimes we don't let him, so we think of substitutes. For instance, one compromise we made was to keep the regular family photo album apart and then create one just for him. It is full of all the not-so-great pictures we left out of the grown-up album, but it is lots of fun for him. He loves to have things like Mom and Dad have. Sometimes we will alter the album just for fun and add cut-out magazine pictures and stickers.

I stand by the time-tested favorite toy, the cardboard box. It's cheap and fun. When I was a kid, I played with cardboard boxes more than almost any other toy. There are so many uses for a box. From babies to teenagers, kids love to hide in them, crawl under them, and make trains and tables out of them. When they are older, they love to make forts (my personal favorite). Even when your kids are too old to play, boxes can be used for storage or for bills.

The computer is a such a wonderful invention! When I have time in the evenings, I download clipart from the Internet and print it out. My kids love to color them or cut them out and stick them on the wall.

Sometimes I will use my child's drawings or photographs to make new games. For example, I cut them up into pieces and create a new puzzle for him to play with.

We didn't want to spend a lot of money decorating our baby's room, but we didn't want to leave it with plain, boring, white walls, either. While at a baby furniture store, I found an inexpensive and very practical solution: a colorful border in a roll that sticks on with the same sort of adhesive backing as on Post-it notes. It was very simple to unroll the border at an eye-catching height along the walls. We chose an under-the-sea theme, but the store also sold sets in other themes, such as wild west, dinosaurs, the circus, and jungle animals. The decorating kit came with many additional stick-on sea creatures that we could arrange around the border any way we liked. The best thing about it is that when the baby is older and ready for a more grown-up room design, we can simply peel off the entire set, and the walls are left unmarked.

Save the empty cardboard rolls from used gift wrap, paper towels, and toilet paper. They're always useful for art projects. Draw a face and a mane on a gift-wrap roll, and you've got an instant hobbyhorse for a toddler. A paper towel roll can turn into an elephant's trunk, and two used toilet rolls held together with rubber bands will make the binoculars for the big-game hunter to use to spot the elephant. Take five empty toilet-paper rolls and one used paper-towel roll to construct a giraffe: Use four of the toilet rolls for the legs and one for the body, and the paper-towel roll becomes the neck, with a bit at the end cut out and folded over to make the head. Use yarn for a tail and a mane. Paint or color with markers, and you're done.

It's very easy to make a dress-up trunk for little girls. Save a really big cardboard carton (like the one your new microwave came in). Cover it in gold or silver foil wrapping paper. If it doesn't open on the wide side, use a utility knife to cut the wide side and create a good lid. Tape up any loose flaps with decorative tape. Use adhesive Velcro strips to make a closure. Fill it with old satin slips (modified if necessary for smaller waists), old hats, gloves, silk scarves, anything with sequins, costume jewelry, high-heeled shoes, purses, and other accessories. If you decide to buy a few items to go in the dress-up trunk, don't go to the toy store—you'll find many more choices for much less money at a fabric store. You can buy lengths of feathered trim to make a boa, or fake-fur cloth to make a stole, or almost anything else your child fancies. Take her with you and let her help you with the sewing projects, and you'll both have fun.

~❀~

We started taking our children to the library when they were just crawling babies. The children's section has a basket of indestructible board books, and so from an early age they came to see the library as a place to sit and have fun with books. Now on any rainy afternoon when we're looking for something to do, one of them will always suggest a visit to the library.

~❀~

Here's a good new-baby present that's different from the usual clothes and stuffed animals. Save the newspaper on the day the baby is born. Cut out any interesting headlines (avoiding those that are gory or depressing), cut out the weather map for the day (especially from a full-color newspaper, such as *USA Today*), and collect various pictures and memorabilia from the top movies, CDs, books, and magazines of the moment. Movie ads, cut-outs from a book jacket or a CD cover, baseball cards or sports scoreboxes, or photos of celebrities are all good ways of capturing the spirit of the baby's birthday. You might also want to include the day's horoscope from the paper, a bit of a comic strip, or the Dow-Jones report (but only if it's been a good day). Glue these clippings and what-not to a cloth-covered piece of plyboard or a piece of poster board in an artistic arrangement. You might want to cover the whole collage with a layer of varnish to seal everything in place. It's wise to use a standard size of board so you can buy a ready-made mat and frame for it. Add hanging hardware, and you've got a custom-made work of art to commemorate the baby's birth.

Photocopy centers or film-developing stores now can usually handle transfers of photographs to cloth. A good gift for grandparents is a t-shirt with photos of all the grandchildren's faces arranged in a semicircle. You can also use indelible markers and fabric paint to add each grandchild's name and birth date to the shirt or paint a tree-trunk with branches and leaves around each photo to make a "family tree."

Egg cartons have any number of kid-friendly uses. They make excellent palettes for color-mixing of poster paints. They help a child sort and store coins, small seashells, rocks, marbles, or tiny toys. They can be cut and decorated to resemble caterpillars or centipedes. You can use them as targets for a bean-tossing game (with different point values for hitting different egg compartments), and if you get the Styrofoam type that's waterproof, you can use them as bathtub toys or boats. Later on, when you have a teenager who likes to play the electric guitar at top volume at midnight, you can line the teenager's walls from floor to ceiling with the egg cartons, and they make excellent sound baffles.

I keep a box on hand full of sewing notions, colored and sparkly glues in tubes, pipe cleaners, fabric markers, old scraps of fabric, buttons, and other odds and ends for all kinds of art projects. I've found you can buy little packages of eyes in different sizes at any crafts store, and any time you've got an old sock, glue some eyes on, paint on nostrils, add pipe cleaners for antennae, or legs, and you've made a puppet! Kids really love the toys and puppets they've made themselves the best.

SHOPPING

Shopping can be the activity kids hate the most. Who wants to spend all day being dragged around by Mom? Here, moms give suggestions on how to keep shopping trips brief and make them easier on both mother and child.

Shopping with a small child is tough, but some stores have gone a long way toward making it easier. My local supermarket has baby-sized shopping carts, so my four-year-old can push her tiny cart along as I push my big one. I always put the cookies and juice and other grocery items that are for her in her smaller cart. For babies, the store also has carts with built-in infant seats. And of course, we always head for the check-out aisle with the big hanging sign that says, "Parents, there is no candy displayed at this check-out." If your store doesn't have such a designated aisle, lobby them until they create one.

I've learned from experience: Never take a hungry child to the grocery store. Give them some snacks to bring from home in a Ziploc bag so they won't demand that you buy them every brand of cookie on the shelf.

~∞~

I always shop with a list when I have my children with me. That way I don't get distracted by their questions and suggestions and forget an item or bring home things I don't really want. Also, whenever they point to candy or other junk foods, I just hand them the list and say, "Where do you see that written?" And with six- and seven-year-olds, letting them read your list also helps teach them to read.

~∞~

I find that grocery shopping with my three children can be the lowest point of my week. I dreaded going into the store and having my children beg me to buy them things, which I used to give in to. My sister — a mother herself — suggested this, and it works for both of us. I let each one of my children pick out one item that they can put into the grocery cart, and that's it. My kids get excited about all the possibilities, but because they can only take one thing, they're not overwhelmed by the choices. This makes for a much easier trip to the store.

~∞~

Whenever I take the baby marketing with me, I ask the checker to bag all my perishables, milk and meats and frozen foods, in the same bag. That way, when I get home, I can carry my baby and that one bag in from the car in one trip. After I've put away all the foods that need to stay cold, I can take my time to get my baby settled down for a nap or feed him lunch in his high chair without needing to rush back to the car to unload the other bags.

Say you are going to the mall. Shopping with toddlers can be exhausting, so be prepared. Make sure you have packed a little grab bag of snacks (for child and mom). Even if you have had a large breakfast, it's better to be safe than sorry. Try to shop in segments. Go to a few of the stores you absolutely need to go to, starting at the point farthest away and working your way back home. This way, both of you won't get tired out, and when it's over, mom and child are the closest to home they can be. Toys and a stroller are also essentials! Don't leave home without them!

TRANSPORTATION

Getting your child from the house to the grocery store may be a little harder than it looks. You have to tackle the car seat first! Then, once you have arrived at your destination, how will you get little Johnny around? For some parents, car-seat and stroller struggles bring out the worst in their little angels and push parental patience to the limit. In this section, moms compare helpful car-seat strategies for getting toddlers ready to travel.

I bought a front-and-back model stroller, and it has been worth every cent. The back lies right down for the baby to sleep, and the front can lie down too, which is great as a changing table when we go swimming at the local pool as a family. The side-by-side models are hard to get around shops with. Back-and-front style makes the stroller longer but much more accessible. Ours has 4x dual wheels, which give great steering, and a huge shopping basket the whole length of the pram, which is much needed. Just try phoning or visiting baby shops in your area until you find one that sells this model.

~❦~

The safest place to install a baby's car seat is in the center of the back seat, but then the problem is, how do you know what's wrong when your baby is crying? I found a mirror that can be safely clipped to the top of the back seat and angled so that you can see your baby's reflection in your rearview mirror. Now when my baby has spit up or lost hold of his teddy, I know what the trouble is and can safely pull over and fix it.

~❦~

It was easy to get our daughter to sleep on car trips when she was still a baby in a car seat. The car seat was slightly tilted and had cushioned supports around the top and sides so that she could lean her head comfortably to one side, as on a pillow. But now that she's outgrown her car seat and just wears a seat belt, it's been much more difficult to get her to fall asleep in the car. When she drifts off, her head flops to one side, making her uncomfortable, and she wakes up. However, I found two possible solutions that both work quite well. For a child still young enough to use a booster seat, you can buy the type that supports the whole body and, just like a toddler car seat, provides a head support to make sleeping in the car more comfortable. For older children who have outgrown boosters, you can buy a self-supporting U-shaped neck pillow. These are typically sold in luggage stores and aimed at adults who take long airplane trips. The cheapest type is inflatable, but the more comfortable ones are filled with bean-bag stuffing or sand. Having a place to rest her head has made my daughter quite willing to go off on long drives with us that she used to dread.

As the mother of five, I've been through a lot of strollers in my time and seen a lot of design changes in the past fifteen years, but the innovation that has been the most helpful is the invention of the combination stroller–infant car seat. The stroller is actually just a frame with wheels and a handle, and you snap the baby's car seat into the frame. When you want to put the baby in the car, you take the whole seat out of the stroller, fold up the frame, and pop the car seat into its base (which is already per-manently installed in your car). The main advantage to this is that you can transfer your sleeping baby from stroller to car and back without ever waking her up.

I have an idea about putting the child in the car seat. I have seen a lot of my friends struggling with children as they try to do this, because the kids don't like the seats. I don't want to fight with my one-year-old daughter! So after I purchased the car seat, I didn't put it in the car.

Instead, I put it in the living room. I told my kid that it was her chair. I made her sit in the car seat every day. She was happy that she got her own chair! Two weeks later, I told her that I was going to put her seat in the car, so that she could have a better view. Naturally, she agreed, and we never had any problem!

My son suddenly got fussy a couple weeks ago when we put him in his car seat. I looked, and he had outgrown the way the straps were set. I loosened them, and we had no more problems.

TRAVEL

Are we there yet? Parents will do almost anything to avoid hearing those words. Many age-old games, singalongs, and travel tactics have been used and proven ineffective at best. Kids get bored anyway, and when they do, watch out! We have all had the unfortunate experience of sitting next to an unhappy child on an airplane or being the mother of that child pushed to her limit. But the trip is only half the battle. Once the family arrives at their final destination, where will the little ones sleep? How well will they deal with family activities? In this section, moms answer sticky questions and offer alternatives for these tough situations.

Try a spin on the old car-trip games like punch buggy, where kids try to spot particular things. Punch buggy can get a little violent with children, though, so change the rules a little. You don't want children hitting each other in the arm every time they spot a Volkswagen bug. Decide on a few items to keep an eye out for, like girls with hats or yellow trucks, things that are hard to find. When the object is seen, you yell it out. Once they are all found, it's time to start over again. It's usually really fun for all of us.

⟨✤⟩

This works for long car trips. Everybody in the car gets cash. Whenever there is complaining about when we are going to get there or how long it is taking, that person has to pay back some money. Believe me, Mom also has to pay if she starts complaining. This works because it keeps everyone in the car, parents and kids, aware of their actions.

⟨✤⟩

One good idea for traveling often or with a family is to buy brightly colored luggage. This makes life easy when sifting through a sea of black luggage.

⟨✤⟩

Once, when traveling cross-country with my family, I set up a special game gift set for each of my kids for the ride. I surprised them with it the morning of the trip. Each gift set was a different color, containing fun little items that were only that color. The two girls got red and blue, and the boy got a green set. Inside were all kinds of pens and stickers, colored pencils and notepads, a rubber stamp with their names on it, and ink pads. Because I gave it to them only that morning, they felt it was their really special travel pack, which made it more fun. They were thrilled. I also gave each one of them a map of the U.S. in their bags so they could mark the trip with their colored pencils. If you are looking for travel items, try Rand McNally atlases or any of the stores in the mall specializing in travel. They usually have all kinds of fun little gifts for kids and adults!

~⟋⟍∘

We have baby gates in our house to keep our crawling son from toppling downstairs, but there are plenty of times we need stairway protection when we're away from home. We rent a vacation house for two weeks every year — and then there are weekly visits to the grandparents and occasional weekend stays with other relatives and friends. The answer is a portable gate. Gerry makes a mesh gate that can be pressure-mounted to any stairway or doorway from twenty-seven to forty-two inches wide. It rolls up for storage in your car trunk until you need it again.

~⟋⟍∘

When packing your carry-on bag for an airplane trip, don't forget lots of snacks. You never know when the flight could be delayed, and you could end up sitting on the runway for an hour or more. Flight attendants usually won't serve any food or drinks while you're waiting — and you can't go back to the terminal to get any, either. I've learned that a few drink boxes and bags of crackers or pretzels can make the difference between the flight from hell and the flight that was merely overly long.

~⊛~

When staying at a friend's vacation house, we worried about how to make the large back deck secure so that our toddler wouldn't fall through the widely spaced railings. A neighbor gave us a spool of neon-green fishing line, which worked wonderfully well. We tied the line to the post where the railing began and wove it between the handrail and the deck boards till we'd filled in all the gaps. Our vacation was much more relaxing after that, and before we left, we rewound the fishing line back onto the spool, and it was still usable for fishing.

~⊛~

Why not to choose bulkhead seating: Sure, there is some extra floor space and no one seated directly in front of you, *but* the arm rests don't raise, making seating uncomfortable at times. Trays pull out of the arm rests and make it impossible to feed a child on your lap. There's no storage for the carry-on you will need constantly with all the stuff you planned to use to entertain the child, making you get up and fetch every time you need something. Sometimes the bulkhead area is the path to the restroom, which makes it dangerous for your child to be on the floor, blocking the path. One time, the serving cart was parked in front of us the entire trip, filled with hot coffee and the like. An unnerving ride for me.

⚬

Sometimes the greatest games are the simplest. When traveling by plane, try giving your kids one empty cup and one cup full of ice. They love to chew on the ice and pour the ice chips from one cup to another. The best part is, it's mess-free.

⚬

Bring a travel pack for kids on road trips. You can create a makeshift one from items in your home. Bring a rectangular cake pan with a slide-on lid, coloring books, paper, new crayons, and the like. The pan acts as a travel desk, and the items can be stored inside!

⚬

I'm concerned about the lack of air safety that many parents practice. Use a proper child seat when flying and always have a separate seat for your child. Don't share! We practice safety in a car, don't we?

⚬

On any long trip, we try to bring lots of audio tapes for the kids to listen to. We get a wide range of subject matter so they have a variety to choose from. Poetry, scary stories, and comedy routines all help pass the time and are really educational.

⚬

When traveling with a baby, make sure to bring a change of clothes not only for your child but for yourself. Over-pack formulas and diapers. But even if you do run out of diapers, many airport shops have handy single-set travel packs. One rule of thumb for dressing: layers, layers, lay-ers! Traveling can take you through many different weather systems and climates, not only outside but from airport to airport and plane to plane. Make sure you and your baby dress appropriately.

Most hotels and motels will set up cribs or cots for your children if you call in advance and request it. But I've found that if you ask for a crib at the time you make the reservation, you'll just have to ask again when you check in. To make sure that the crib is set up and ready in the room when you arrive, call about two to three hours be-fore you expect to get there. That way, if your baby is ready to nap, you will avoid a long and sometimes frus-trating delay.

When you go on long-distance drives with your baby, avoid doing diaper changes at one of those big public rest stops with their overused, poorly maintained changing ta-bles. Your baby probably won't feel comfortable in a huge, crowded bathroom, and neither will you. For those who have a minivan or station wagon, you may find that the opened tailgate makes an excellent changing table in warm weather. Keep a roll of trash bags in the back of your car so that you can dispose of the old diaper and used wipes after the baby has been cleaned up.

We had the commonly experienced problem of how to make sure our five-year-old child could ride safely in taxis or in the cars of friends or relatives who did not have booster seats. The solution we found is a nylon sleeve called SafeFit that adjusts the ordinary shoulder-and-lap belt so that it will effectively restrain a small child. Without the SafeFit, the shoulder belt crosses over a child's neck and could possibly do more harm than good in an accident. The SafeFit is inexpensive, very portable, and easy enough for a child to learn to put on properly by himself. We've been a lot less worried about our son's visits to his grandparents and rides home from school with friends since he's had his SafeFit. We got ours through a catalog called The Safety Zone (1-800-999-3030).

We've found the easiest way to manage a long car trip with small children is to begin the drive right around the children's bedtime. We put them in their pajamas, strap them into their car seats, and hit the road. Within a half an hour they're fast asleep, and we can usually count on them to stay that way until we reach our destination the next morning. My husband and I trade off driving duties and sleep time in the passenger seat, and we both try to get in a few long naps the following day, so we're not sleep-deprived at the start of our vacation.

When we didn't have a Pack N Play pen on trips, we used the second bed in a room with two beds and made a "pen" of pillows . . . one on each side of baby and one at the head and foot. That way, it was too hard for my daughter to roll out. Of course, as she got older, we just made a pallet on the floor and penned it in. The space between two beds in a hotel works great. Just push a chair in the end to block it off and use lots of blankets to keep the baby from rolling under the bed and from hitting his head on the bed rails.

WORDS OF WISDOM

Moms leave us with little tips and tricks they have learned on the road of parenthood.

Trust your instincts. Even if the experts don't agree with you. When it comes to your kids, you are the expert because no one knows them as well as you do.

⁓🙖

Call before you go.
Call before you bundle up baby and nurse baby
and realize baby needs a change and change baby
and bundle up baby and get baby into car seat and
clean up spit up on your shoulder and drive
to the store to find out that they are out of
what you came for . . .

⁓🙖

One of my biggest pieces of advice would be to tell first-time mothers not to focus too much on the labor and birth part of the experience but on all that comes soon after. I felt that my child prep classes and overall pregnancy "input" was mostly focused on the birth process. Although I am a reasonably intelligent person with a good amount of common sense and was anticipating the difficulties I'd encounter when coming home with the new baby, I ran into problems I hadn't really anticipated that I understand now are very common (example: problems with breastfeeding; it's never emphasized that it can be difficult and that it's not just a "natural" or easy thing for all women).

Before you go to the doctor and find he is running three hours late, giving you three hours to expose baby to all those sick kids ... Before you go *anywhere*, before you even dress baby to go out, *call*!

I have only one piece of advice: Hold your children and rock and love them with your entire heart and soul. You don't need to "train them" to grow up—all that's required is your love. The speed of time is about to increase to a rate you never would have believed. Make every precious moment count. Listen well, but let your heart be your guide. Trust yourself.

A few years ago I found myself and my nursing infant traveling one hot summer day with my sister and her young children (none of whom were still nursing). Well, we stopped in a parking lot to change the youngest one's diapers and so I could nurse my baby. One of my nephews, about four years old, looked on while I nursed discreetly. After a moment or two, he asked his mother, "What's she doing?" My sister replied, "Feeding the baby." Once again a question came, "What's she feeding the baby?" My sister answered, "Milk." My nephew looked at me again, then back at his mother and then back at me and finally looked at his mother and asked, "Does she have any apple juice in there?"